Endorsements for Todd Duncan's *Life on the Wire*

"I've always believed that when you're at work, you should work hard, and when you're at home, you should play hard. That's easy to say, but for a lot of people it's hard to do. In *Life on the Wire*, Todd Duncan clears up the myth about the 'balanced' life and shows you how to rejoice in the purposeful— and planned—imbalanced life."

Dave Ramsey
Best-selling author and host of
the Dave Ramsey Show

"There are a whole lot of people driving themselves crazy trying to 'live a balanced life.' You and I know it doesn't work! Todd Duncan's new book shows us what *does* work! How to transform natural imbalance into harmony! A must read!"

— Bob Beaudine
best-selling author,
The Power of WHO

"This book quickly shows you how to get more done, of greater importance, and less time, and dramatically increase the quality of your entire life."

— Brian Tracy
Best-selling author and
professional speaker

"Todd has really touched on an important perspective regarding 'Life Balance.' I love his concept of purposeful imbalance! Timely and relevant . . . reading this book will give you a nice bit of personal peace."

— Terri Sjodin
principle and founder, Sjodin
Communications

"Anyone suffering from frustration or a feeling of hopelessness as a result of buying the all-too-common lie that 'they will get to it tomorrow when things slow down' has to read *Life On The Wire*. Our life's story will not be defined by one single decision, but instead, by the little daily decisions that, when combined, will create our legacy. Read it today."

— Daniel Harkavy
CEO and Executive Coach,
Building Champions, Inc. and
author of *Becoming a Coaching Leader*

"A *simple truth* is that when you have faith in your future, you can have power in your present. *Life on the Wire* will show you how to manage the tension in every facet of your life so you can live and work more effectively and enjoy both more abundantly."

— Mac Anderson
founder of Simple Truths and
Successories and author of
The Nature of Success

"Powerful life experiences often give you life-changing wisdom. Todd has had both! Open these pages and discover practical yet potent advice for pursuing your dreams and living your life well!"

— Glenna Salsbury
CSP, CPAE, speaker Hall of
Fame, author of *The Art of the Fresh Start* and *Professional Speaker*

"Everyone who lives on the wire of wanting to do more, have more, be more, and contribute more will appreciate how Todd's advice can help you make that happen while navigating the mental challenges that accompany the choice to live a BIG life."

— Bill Bachrach,
CSP, CPAE, CEO of BAI and
author of *Values-Based Financial Planning*

LIFE
ON THE
WIRE

Avoid Burnout and Succeed
in Work and Life

TODD DUNCAN

THOMAS NELSON
Since 1798

NASHVILLE   DALLAS   MEXICO CITY   RIO DE JANEIRO

© 2010 by McLean Taylor, Inc.

Published in Nashville, Tennessee by Thomas Nelson. Thomas Nelson is a registered trademark of Thomas Nelson, Inc.

Page design: Walter Petrie

Published in association with Yates & Yates, LLP, www.yates2.com.

Thomas Nelson, Inc. titles may be purchased in bulk for educational, business, fund-raising, or sales promotional use. For information, please e-mail SpecialMarkets@ThomasNelson.com.

Unless otherwise noted, Scripture quotations are taken from the HOLY BIBLE: NEW INTERNATIONAL VERSION®. © 1973, 1978, 1984 by International Bible Society. Used by permission of Zondervan Publishing House. All rights reserved.

Scripture quotations marked NASB are from the NEW AMERICAN STANDARD BIBLE®, © The Lockman Foundation 1960, 1962, 1963, 1968, 1971, 1972, 1973, 1975, 1977, 1995. Used by permission.

ISBN 978-1-59555-526-7 (TP)

Library of Congress Cataloging-in-Publication Data

Duncan, Todd, 1957–
    Life on the wire : avoid burnout and succeed in work and life / by Todd Duncan.
        p. cm.
    Includes bibliographical references.
    ISBN 978-0-7852-1898-2
    1. Quality of work life. 2. Job satisfaction. 3. Burn out (Psychology)—Prevention. I. Title.
    HD6955.D856 2009
    650.1—dc22   2009033800

Printed in the United States of America

FOR MY WIFE, SHERYL

THE HUMOR, COURAGE, LOVE, GENEROSITY,
AND FAITH YOU DEMONSTRATED AS YOU
WALKED THE WIRE ARE AN INSPIRATION TO
ANYONE WHO WANTS TO FACE THE BATTLE
AND FINISH LIFE STRONG. YOU WERE AN
AMAZING WIFE AND A PHENOMENAL MOM
AND YOU WILL NEVER BE FORGOTTEN!
THANK YOU FOR MAKING A DIFFERENCE.
I LOVE YOU, FOREVER!

SHERYL B. DUNCAN
FEBRUARY 5, 1958 – SEPTEMBER 4, 2009

WWW.SHERYLDUNCANFOREVER.COM

CONTENTS

CONTENTS

FOREWORD

I n *Life on the Wire*, my friend Todd Duncan turns the world of balance upside down and inside out. The result is a totally refreshing, truly invigorating, and thoroughly convincing new formula for work-life success.

Truth be told, we are all on the wire. Haven't you felt the pressure of performing without a net? Hasn't life dealt you tough choices? Have there been days you thought you might not even make it? If you are like me, then you've missed deadlines on important projects, tried in vain to deflect stress, experienced the agony of leaving home for work, and even the fear of leaving work for home!

Perhaps you have had to decide between a boss's request to attend a strategic planning session and your son's first baseball game or your daughter's first piano recital. Maybe the challenge at hand is making ends meet in today's difficult financial times. Or perhaps your spouse told you he or she didn't love you anymore, and you felt the whole "wire" oscillate.

We have all experienced the consternation that seems to inhabit quests for success. In these pages, however, my charge for you is simple: travel with Todd from cover to cover. You won't be sorry you took the trip. This book will help you achieve a more balanced life and place you firmly on the road to achieving much more than mere success. With the assistance of these well-thought-out points, well-told stories, and the application of timeless principles, your life will become one of significance!

At this point in your life (and why *did* you pick up this book?), you probably already know that neither conquest, power, nor the acquisition of material things will produce lasting joy or fulfillment. In fact, when we finally complete the achievements we thought would create significance and happiness in our lives, we often realize that those achievements produced the opposite effect of what was intended! For many, success hasn't produced contentment; it has simply forced us farther out on "the wire," demanding that we achieve even more.

I believe that the quality of our answers can only be determined by the quality of our questions. In this, the search you are about to begin to create the life of your dreams, allow me to pose a few: How would you live if this were your last month on earth? Would you consider the things you have accomplished thus far significant? Where would you spend the majority of your time? With whom? What would your legacy be?

I am not suggesting that success is not important. It is. But for one to create a life of fulfillment and significance, success cannot be the only target for which we aim. In these pages, Todd will propose a new and radical style of work—an extreme makeover for your life on and off the job. He'll also demonstrate, through a series of *Tension Points,* how you can manage the daily decisions that have the power to alter your life experience forever.

I believe you will find this to be one of the best books ever written on work-life success. Grab a highlighter, dig in, and expect to find a brand new balance in your *Life on the Wire!*

—Andy Andrews
New York Times Bestselling Author of
The Traveler's Gift and *The Noticer*

The Art of Purposeful Imbalance

F amed tightrope walker Tino Wallenda and his family, the Flying
Wallendas, have been walking on high wires without nets for nearly
a century. When asked how he maintains balance on a wire with nothing but earth beneath him, Tino gently corrects the assumption: "The
reality is that you are never actually balanced; you are constantly making small adjustments—moving back and forth—and it's those constant
movements that keep you on the wire. The truth is, if you stand still,
you fall."

The same is true of harmonizing our personal and professional
worlds. You are never actually balanced, *nor should you try to be*. To
ensure a more harmonious existence, you must keep yourself moving—carefully teetering and tottering between work and life activities.
Like a tightrope walker, you must regularly make adjustments back
and forth to keep yourself standing. The key is being purposeful, having sound reasons for everything you do.

Many of these purposeful adjustments are small and require mere
acts of personal discipline. For example:

- Leaving work at a set time each day
- Carving out thirty minutes every other day for a jog
- Reserving one lunch a week for connecting with friends

Occasionally, the adjustments are bigger and require greater sacrifice. For example:

- Finding a new job with a shorter commute
- Cutting back to part time to be a better parent
- Taking a new position within your company in exchange for a more flexible schedule

The point is that both big and small adjustments are inevitably necessary to maintain work/life harmony. Instead of aiming for equitable division of your work/life time, strive for purposeful give-and-take. Give more time to work this week since that report is due on Friday, in return for more time for your personal life next week. Or, give more time to your personal life during the next two months—to be with your new baby—in return for more time for work during the following months.

Eventually the season will change, and you will return to some of the things you were forgoing. But something else will always come up. This is the natural flow of harmonious living: giving and taking, back and forth between personal and professional activities. Thus, *purposeful imbalance*—not perfect balance—is the only way you can achieve a gratifying work life without decimating your personal life, and a gratifying personal life without abandoning your career aspirations.

The Significance of Snorkeling

The truth of this concept—purposeful imbalance—really hit home with me one day not long ago when my writer, Brent Cole, and I were ensconced in my office, brainstorming the outline for a new book. Brent was staring out the window at the bay as I paged through the spread of articles, clippings, and research we'd gathered during the last two years.

A trio of snorkelers meandered about the shimmering cove, faces down and snorkels protruding above the surface. They glided along the water on this crisp California morning, swimming together and then apart, and were in no hurry in any direction. Occasionally one would stop kicking to bob in place and laugh with one of the others.

"Look down there," Brent said without turning around. "What do you see?"

"What? The water?" I asked as I joined him at the window.

"No, *in* the water."

"The people?"

"Yeah, but what are they doing?"

"They're snorkeling."

"Right. It's ten on a Tuesday morning, and those three are snorkeling. I wonder what they do for a living that they can go snorkeling right now."

Were the three retired? It was possible but unlikely. The two men and one woman looked young, in their thirties at most.

Maybe they were on vacation? Again, possible but unlikely. While the cove was a popular spot during summer months, this was late fall, and the water was around sixty degrees. The only people down there now were most likely locals. Certainly, the three were enthusiasts—but vacationers? That was doubtful.

Were they among the many newly unemployed? Perhaps, but they didn't seem to have a care in the world that morning.

What sort of jobs did they have? What sort of families? Obligations? Responsibilities? Did they enjoy their days as much as it appeared?

Fifteen minutes later, as we were thumbing through the stacks of research back at the meeting table, Brent noticed the snorkelers on the move. Our curiosity getting the better of us, we put down the stacks and watched.

Each man dumped his gear into a nearby car, grabbed a duffel bag, and walked toward the cement building that housed the restrooms and showers. The woman stood next to her SUV. She stepped out of her wetsuit, toweled off, and pulled on sweats and a T-shirt. Sitting sideways in the driver's seat, with her legs dangling above the running board, she poked at a BlackBerry. After a brief call she checked her watch and then swung her legs inside and drove off.

Shortly thereafter, one man reemerged from the shower house, and a minute later, the other man appeared. The first wore a white button-down with the sleeves rolled and black pants and shoes. The second wore a tie, dark slacks, and dress shoes. We could only guess, but it appeared the first was off to wait tables and the other to a corporate office.

Seeking Balance

As the refreshed snorkelers went about their workdays, we paused during ours and asked, *What have they figured out that we haven't?* How does one engage in a gratifying career without missing out on life? If the secret is as simple as making time each week for activities we enjoy, why aren't more of us doing it? Busyness is part of the problem, but we also know being busy isn't a bad thing if we're doing things we enjoy. The real problem is that we invest *too much time* in things we don't love and *not enough time* in the things we do.

We all have activities like snorkeling that we wish were part of our days but which for various reasons remain on hold—even simple pastimes like reading, exercising, or gardening. According to a study in *Fast Company* magazine, 88 percent of American workers admit they struggle to achieve "balance."[2]

As the economy tanks, more and more of us find ourselves working harder than ever as we try to do our own jobs plus the work of our laid-off coworkers. As a result, our days feel tense and rushed, making it a challenge to relish anything.

And then there are the workaholics—people like me not so long ago—for whom activities like a midmorning snorkel, an afternoon bike ride, or a world-traveling hiatus aren't even on the radar. The tension can be so oppressive. At the same time, activities like a midmorning snorkel sound enchanting, even *necessary*, no matter how full our workweek. Most of us need them far more than a raise or promotion or new set of circumstances.

In fact, if enjoyable, life-giving activities were routine, you'd feel more energy and less tension.[3] You'd be more grateful for what you have and, on the whole, more delightful to be around. Most important of all, you'd have perspective. With an unflustered outlook on your life, you can seize good opportunities, make the right adjustments, handle success, survive failure, love well, and allow yourself to be well loved.

This is a book about reviving those perspective-giving pastimes you greatly want and need to round out your life. On the whole, it's about how to become more *purposefully balanced*, to have a way of life that facilitates gratification both on and off the job.

An Emerging Trend

Two weeks after the meeting with Brent, I found myself staring out the bay window again. It was earlier this time, about 8:30 a.m., and there was only one snorkeler in the water. I recognized him as the man who wore the tie.

I glanced at my watch and then back at the cove. There was still time before my nine o'clock call. I stood up from my chair, slipped on my flip-flops, and stepped outside. I walked to the end of the hall, down some stairs between my building and the next, and then jogged across the narrow street rimming the cove where the snorkeler was coming ashore. I hopped down the concrete stairs and onto the sand, then approached him as he removed his mask.

I introduced myself and confessed to admiring his friends and him two weeks earlier. "It looked as if you were headed off to work after you finished snorkeling," I said. "Do you work here in town?"

"I do," he replied. "I work for a mortgage company."

I asked him what company, and he told me. I knew the one.

"If you don't mind my asking," I said, "What does your boss think of you snorkeling during work hours?"

He replied, "I was just honest with him, I guess. My last job for [a firm in downtown San Diego] was miserable. I was expected to be in the office all the time. It got to the point where I didn't even have a social life outside of work, so eventually I got some [guts] and quit. So when I started this job, I asked my boss what was more important to him: that I sat in the office a certain number of hours or that I did good work? He said, between me and him, he didn't care about my office hours as long as I met my goals."

"Did your fellow snorkelers do something similar?"

"Sort of. The other guy—James—he's a waiter. He's been there long enough that they let him set his own schedule. The girl you saw works for an event planning company. They let her work from home as long as everything gets done."

"Do you know a lot of people doing this type of thing—arranging for a more flexible work environment?" I asked.

"Definitely more now than maybe five years ago. I think more people have become impatient about waiting for the kind of life they really want." He added emphatically, "They don't want to wait until they're too old to enjoy it."

The snorkeler and I talked a minute more and then said goodbye. I thanked him for the impromptu interview and promised I wouldn't reveal his name. He was worried his boss might not like their arrangement as much if he knew too many details.

Training the Tension

A recent study showed that nearly 75 percent of us admit the need to reduce our work/life tension.[4] Yet, less than 25 percent of us do anything about it. Why is that?

I believe it has a lot to do with a prominent feeling of powerlessness. We don't feel we possess the proper resources—enough money, time, flexibility, or the ideal circumstances—to manage a gratifying work life *and* a rewarding personal life. And so we choose to pursue one or the other. Fortunately, the choice to work *or* to live is not our only option.

The first step toward work/life harmony has less to do with how well you use your time and more to do with *how clearly you see the spectrum of choices before you* and *how willing you are to accommodate your preferences*, personally and professionally.

Jason Lacy is a good example of this. He is a twenty-nine-year-old entrepreneur who recently moved from Miami to San Diego to work with his brother and his childhood best friend. The opportunity offers great potential but no guarantees, and it has little to do with his previous eight years of work. Some friends see the decision as impulsive, but Jason sees a much greater risk in missing out on a once-in-a-lifetime opportunity.

Stories like his suggest that achieving more harmonious days requires a willingness to make choices that may seem to be counterproductive. In generations past, people typically chose a career path and stayed on it because changing course was deemed irresponsible, even dishonorable. Many of us were raised around this mind-set and are consequently (and often subconsciously) blinded to the full spectrum of choices before us—choices that can move us much closer to a wholly gratifying existence; choices that are, in fact, more responsible than remaining stressed out and dissatisfied.

With a much wider sea of opportunities before you than your

predecessors, you make a mistake by accepting limp or oppressive circumstances in the name of duty. You have more opportunities to achieve work/life harmony than you realize. Often the opportunities lie within the realm of your current situation. Sometimes they don't. But they require a choice every time: you must be shrewd enough to make the choice and then willing enough to follow through with the necessary adjustments. This is how you begin to retrain your work/life tension toward work/life harmony.

Better, Not Perfect

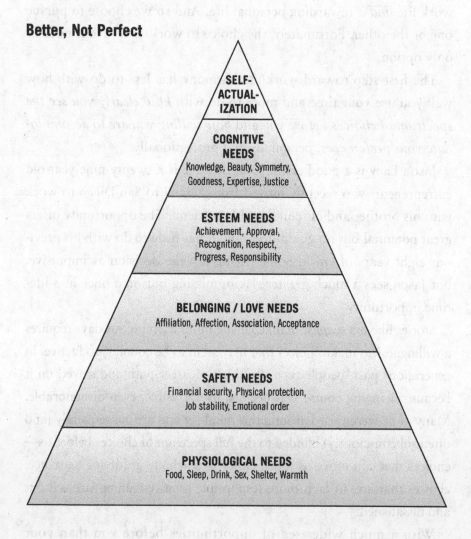

In "A Theory of Human Motivation," his historic paper first published by *Psychological Review* in 1943, American psychologist Abraham Maslow introduced the now-famous pyramid with his premise that once humans can meet basic "physiological needs," such as sleeping, eating, and drinking, we then instinctively seek to satisfy successively higher needs. According to Maslow, the higher the needs you can meet, the more complete or fulfilled you will be. Conversely, if you constantly struggle to meet only the lower needs, you will be less complete or more unfulfilled. Ultimately, each of us instinctively strives to reach the top of the pyramid where self-actualization occurs—where we are the best we can be.

While Maslow's pyramid had its detractors, it remains a foundation in the study of human behavior, and it certainly accounts for the work/life tug-of-war we often feel. What happens is that as we go about addressing our instinctive needs, certain prominent ones come into competition for our time and energy. With only so many hours to meet our needs, there's a high probability that we will lie down at night feeling—but often not understanding—an inner friction we can't kick.

This brings us to the two primary questions we'll answer in the chapters that follow:

- How do you manage each of these various needs without feeling tension?
- How do you know which needs you should meet now and which can wait?

We will find the answers not with a formula for perfect balance but with strategies for purposeful imbalance that will lead to improved work/life harmony.

Imbalance Is Natural—The Key Is to Make It Purposeful

Accepting imbalance as a natural part of your life will give you guilt-free license to focus on certain pressing needs. But you can't guess blindly which needs are most important. You must have a plan for zeroing in on the right needs, or you'll be tempted to use your new mind-set as a cop-out for workaholism, apathy, or indecision. An effective plan includes adopting new practices that allow you to be purposeful about your choices so that you never suffer the consequences of leaning too far in one direction.

Think of purposeful imbalance this way: if you're on a high wire and you lean one way, you can't continue leaning or you'll fall from the wire. Like the Flying Wallendas, you have to know when to lean back the other way . . . and then back the other way . . . and so on, all the while progressing across the wire. The goal of this book is to help you develop a keener sense of how and when to lean back and forth between your predominant needs and still maintain a steady progress in your life.

To reveal how to remain on the work/life high wire and transform its natural imbalance into harmony, I will highlight one common "tension point" in every chapter. I'll illustrate how that particular tension can escalate, and I'll provide the tools you can use to transform it into harmonious imbalance. It's likely you don't struggle at every tension point, but most will be familiar to you from past experience or the current experience of someone you know. This book will not only help you harmonize your days but will also teach you how to help others do the same as well.

"I Have To" vs. "I *Really Want* To"

> One of the things I've learned . . . is to first ask myself, "Do I
> philosophically believe in what I'm doing?" . . . But I also have to
> ask, "Do I get warm fuzzies from what I'm doing?" When I asked
> myself that question my answer was, "No, with this stuff I don't."
> That was a real eye-opener.
>
> —Jason Lacy

J ason Lacy has a strong foundation for success. Raised by an entrepreneur mother and a famous motivator father, he grew up surrounded by tools of inspiration. After putting his self-proclaimed
"idiot years" behind him, he naturally set his sights on starting a
groundbreaking business. Admirable as that vision was, it had to
marinate in the bittersweet broth of experience before finally coming to life. Today Jason sums up the lessons of his last eight years as
a "constant challenge to answer the question, *Am I pursuing the right
objective?*

"I am still always asking, *Is this for the money? Or for the prestige of
being a successful entrepreneur? Or for something I really believe in?*"
Now Jason can answer these questions with a measure of confidence—
though there was a time when his answers didn't come so easily. He
struggled with the tension common to creative and entrepreneurial types

1

that develops when job requirements compete with a passion for work that is emotionally rewarding.

At twenty-two, Jason was clearing six figures as a broker for a small financial services firm in Carmel Valley, California, when a brainstorm began one day during a conversation with a friend. The two of them discovered an underused tax advantage in the lucrative life insurance industry and then composed a plan for creating and marketing new software that would help policyholders utilize it. After raising private funds, both quit their steady jobs and ventured out. You may have considered the same move as you slog through the mire of mundane workdays. The few who take action are those of a rare mind-set, willing to experiment before firming their feet in a job or career. Jason embraced this experimental thinking wholeheartedly.

"It was a great idea," Jason explained of their venture, "but we quickly discovered our product was hard to describe. We kept hearing things like, 'It sounds great but I just don't understand how it works' and 'Why hasn't my financial advisor told me about this?'" After a season of frustration—and nearing the end of their funding—Jason and his business partner morphed their product into something more marketable.

The revised concept was broader in scope and easier to describe, and the adjustments proved lucrative. A large southeastern firm saw the new software's potential and offered to fund its overhead and marketing in exchange for a share of ownership. "From a financial standpoint, it made perfect sense," Jason admitted. "The unspoken reality was that we needed it to happen if we wanted to keep paying our bills."

What Jason didn't immediately see was how the merger would squeeze the vigor out of the venture. Partnering with the large company was a step toward financial stability but away from what he loved about his workdays as an entrepreneur. Jason was unknowingly entering a common tangle.

Most of us reach a point where our initial efforts to land a stable job transition into the desire for an inspiring one. The quest for satisfying, emotionally rewarding workdays generates a natural tension we must harmonize in order to meet our simultaneous needs for job stability and meaningful achievement.

Jason is seeking a rudimentary need in maintaining a steady job while also striving for personal achievement higher up the pyramid.

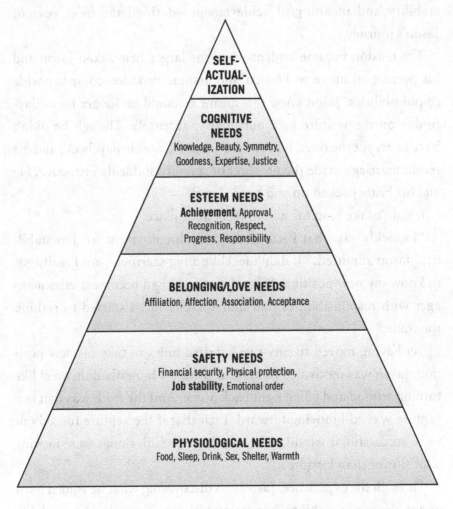

SELF-ACTUAL-IZATION

COGNITIVE NEEDS
Knowledge, Beauty, Symmetry, Goodness, Expertise, Justice

ESTEEM NEEDS
Achievement, Approval, Recognition, Respect, Progress, Responsibility

BELONGING/LOVE NEEDS
Affiliation, Affection, Association, Acceptance

SAFETY NEEDS
Financial security, Physical protection, **Job stability**, Emotional order

PHYSIOLOGICAL NEEDS
Food, Sleep, Drink, Sex, Shelter, Warmth

Here we see the two points of tension. Jason is both seeking a rudimentary need in maintaining a steady job while striving for personal achievement.

The Value of Your Work

Lack of job stability is not only a strain on your well-being but also on the health of your relationships. I've seen it take marriages to the brink of divorce. On the other hand, the consequences of a dreary day's work that never excites you can be just as detrimental. It's hard to say which deficit is more serious. Wrestling with these two needs— stability and meaningful achievement—defined the next year of Jason's journey.

The tension became evident when the larger firm asked Jason and his partner to move to Florida and assume broader, company-wide responsibilities. Jason knew this meant he could no longer focus day-to-day on the venture he'd nurtured so intensely. Though he didn't have to accept the offer, it promised a steady, sizable paycheck, and his recent marriage made the prospect of stability suddenly attractive. He and his bride packed up and headed east.

It didn't take long for him to feel out of place.

"I quickly saw that I had sacrificed job enjoyment for job stability," Jason admitted. "It didn't feel like a big sacrifice until I really got to know my new position. When I realized I had become a sales manager with responsibilities that didn't excite me, I started to rethink the trade."

Yet having moved twenty-five hundred miles to take his new position, Jason was motivated to make it work. "I honestly didn't feel like turning around and going right back home. And the truth was that our venture was still moving forward. I felt that if the venture turned out to be successful, it would all be worth it . . . Still, things were moving a lot slower than I wanted."

Through the experience, Jason was discovering what he valued most about a job: not stability, but seeing his ideas flourish. His work/life tension peaked when he realized his daily responsibilities no longer included pursuing his dream. His workdays fed job stability but starved job gratification.

Jason set a decision deadline. "I told myself I'd stay one year and make the best of it. I knew if I still felt the same after being here a year, I had to make a change—even though I didn't have a clue what that would be."

For months Jason gutted it out in hopes the software venture would bloom under the umbrella of the larger company and his workdays would regain the flexibility, independence, and inspiration he craved. Unfortunately, a few weeks from his anniversary there, he saw but little progress. It was at this point—when doing what was required kept him from doing what was rewarding—that we first spoke to Jason. He was candid about his missteps and the lessons he was still learning. His insights will illuminate the tools for harmonizing your tension in the same area.

A Question of Objectives

"One of the things I've learned about my work pursuits from now on," Jason explained, "is to first ask myself, *Do I philosophically believe in what I am doing?* It's critical to know that, at the end of the day, I actually think what I'm doing is ethical and useful. It makes no sense to spend time doing something you are philosophically at odds with. When I asked myself if I philosophically believed in what I was doing here, my answer was yes. Life insurance is a useful product I can get behind.

"But I've learned that is only half the equation. I also have to ask myself, *Do I get warm fuzzies from what I'm doing?* When I asked myself that question, my answer was, *No, with this particular job I don't.* I can be motivated to do it from a moneymaking standpoint, but ultimately the daily tasks don't inspire me at my core . . . Seeing that was a real eye-opener."

Ultimately, Jason discovered the tension he felt was a result of a misalignment between his work requirements and his work objectives. If that tension point hits home with you, you're probably struggling with the same conflict.

The relationship between your work requirements and work objectives plays a major role in whether you feel tension. If the two are aligned, there is little room for tension—because the end justifies the means. If there is misalignment between them, there's a high potential for tension— because the end does not justify the means.

The various seasons of life lead you to take jobs for different reasons. As long as the requirements of the job promote your work objectives, you're not likely to feel any serious tension. If your current objective is to maintain a predictable schedule and paycheck, you're less likely to feel tension from a lackluster job because it doesn't keep you from reaching your main goal. During another season, however, your primary objective might be emotional gratification, in which case you'd be less willing to accept the same lackluster job because it would be out of alignment with that "higher" (according to Maslow's pyramid) objective.

The first step toward decreasing misalignment and harmonizing the tension between your job requirements and job objectives is to figure out what type of job best fits you and your current circumstances. For the most part, there are two types of jobs: comfortable ones and inspirational ones.

The Comfortable Job

Advantages of a comfortable job include stability, predictability, and a clear path to advancement. Certain seasons of life are ideal for a comfortable job:

- Graduating from college, when your most desirable career path is not yet clear
- Entering a new industry, when you don't yet know if there is philosophical alignment
- Moving to a new city, when you don't yet know if the location suits your and/or your family's needs
- Completing a post-graduate program, when you have large debts to pay off
- Reentering the workforce after having children, while you are navigating how to simultaneously be a parent and an income producer
- When you have large debts for any reason and want to maintain a consistent pay-down strategy to become debt free

There are other situations where a comfortable job might be the best fit, but before you lean that way, be aware that comfortable jobs share these potential drawbacks:

1. *Limited independence.* Most comfortable jobs come with a defined set of responsibilities that dictate your weekly to-dos. While there is usually room for creativity and change, your required work often has little variety.
2. *Limited inspiration.* Many comfortable jobs are not likely to give you warm fuzzies. Their requirements are not ones many people are passionate about. This can make your workday feel more obligatory than gratifying.
3. *Limited flexibility.* While companies are increasingly willing to redefine nine-to-five, many comfortable jobs require standard hours with scant wiggle room, and even that is available only to those who are shrewd (and gutsy) enough to negotiate for it.
4. *Limited advancement options.* In many comfortable jobs, your opportunities for growth or change are limited by company policy

and industry tradition. If the ladder is wrong for you, climbing it
will not be very fulfilling.

Knowing the potential drawbacks will help you decide whether
your circumstances make a comfortable job the right choice. Defaulting
in that direction without also taking a close look at an inspirational
job, however, is unwise and shortsighted. Remember that you'll only
reduce your requirement/reward tension when your work objectives
are aligned with your job requirements. If you want more from work
than just stability, an inspirational job may be the better way to go.

The Inspirational Job

Key advantages of an inspirational job are its infectious enthusiasm,
large growth potential, and emotional gratification. Certain seasons of
life are ideal for an inspirational job:

- Discovering an organization you could happily spend your entire
  career with
- Finding an industry or cause you deeply believe in
- Creating a specialized product or service that demands a focused,
  long-term effort
- Discovering and developing an extraordinary talent with high
  market value
- You can sustain the lifestyle you desire with minimal income (i.e.,
  you have money in the bank or another source of income that
  requires little time commitment)
- You are single with few obligations, financial and otherwise

As is the case with a comfortable job, before you pursue an inspirational job, it's important to weigh the potential drawbacks:

1. *Inconsistent income.* Many inspirational jobs require you to forgo a regular paycheck and depend (at least initially) on outside investment or personal funding. This can be a nerve-wracking time, requiring great patience and unflagging conviction.

2. *Unpredictable hours.* In most inspirational jobs, long days are both rewarding and unavoidable. If you don't have a plan for maintaining your other values, this time requirement will pose a threat to the pillars of your best life. Many workaholics love their jobs but lose their lives along the way.

3. *Higher risk.* Any time you invest the core of who you are into an endeavor, failure feels heavier. If you don't have a strong emotional and spiritual foundation as well as a body of supporters, such disappointment can disenchant you for a long time, sometimes permanently.

4. *Ever-changing responsibilities.* Many inspirational jobs require you to evolve with the venture or organization. You may be a salesperson one week and an accountant the next. While not all inspirational jobs are entrepreneurial in form, most of them require the willingness to cross-train, multitask, and continue learning.

So which is the better choice for you? That depends.

Your Higher Need

Maslow's original pyramid indicated our higher need is for rewarding achievement (or gratification) and thus an inspirational job. This probably holds true for the majority of workers at some point in their lives. But Maslow would likely also indicate that the tension will remain if you completely ignore the lower need for stability to serve the higher one. This incongruity is where Maslow's contemporaries questioned the stringent, stratified form of his pyramid. Most in the field of human behavior now agree that we all have common, ascending needs but believe that we all inherit (by nature) and learn (by nurture) inclinations that cause our pyramid of needs to differ from individual to individual.

In other words, you may naturally have a greater need for an inspirational job (and hence for rewarding achievement) and not feel the sacrifice of stability. On the other hand, financial stability might naturally be your higher need; therefore you aren't inclined to find an inspirational job.

The point is that there is no standard answer for which type of job is better for everyone. You have to determine what's best for you in this season of life, and that hinges on two things:

- *Your current circumstances.* Do you have large debts? Are you entering a new industry? Have you found a cause or company you are passionate about? Have you discovered and developed a unique gift?
- *Your current makeup.* Which way do you naturally lean? Is job stability or rewarding achievement your higher value?

It's important to note that both your circumstances and your makeup can change over the course of your life. For instance, you might have just bought a new home; therefore job stability is a higher need because now you have a big mortgage payment each month. But perhaps two years from now financial leverage will allow you to pursue a job that is more emotionally rewarding.

Note also that not all jobs fit perfectly into one category, but nearly all lean in one direction or the other. While it's possible to have a job with both comfortable elements and inspirational elements, one side or the other will usually predominate. And, again, if the result is tension, you have some adjustments to make—toward greater job stability or toward rewarding achievement. This is where the path to requirement/reward harmony begins.

I recommend using the following quick reference guide at least twice a year to gauge which way you're leaning. If you discover you're on the wrong side, don't panic. There are straightforward, practical steps you can take right away to begin crossing over.

When a Comfortable Job Is Often Best

- ☐ Job stability is currently a higher value than emotional gratification
- ☐ Entering a new industry and unsure if you'll like it
- ☐ Just moved to a new city and unsure if you'll stay
- ☐ Have large debts to pay off, large payments to maintain, or a big purchase on the horizon
- ☐ Just starting a family
- ☐ Entering the workforce and unsure of career direction

When an Inspirational Job Is Often Best

- ☐ Emotional gratification is currently a higher value than job stability
- ☐ Have deep conviction about a particular cause, product, or organization
- ☐ Possess a highly marketable talent/gift
- ☐ Are certain about career direction
- ☐ Have other means of income that free you up to dream and experiment
- ☐ Have a low-maintenance or low-cost lifestyle

Finding Your Harmony

Teetering on the brink of a big decision, Jason finally got the shove he needed. First came news that a financial services giant planned to launch a venture closely related to his. Then, about the same time, Jason received separate calls from his best friend and his brother back home. Both proposed new business ventures and wanted Jason involved. While the opportunities were no guarantee of income, they had a far greater potential to meet his higher need for an inspirational job.

Seeking confirmation for his next move, Jason called his stepfather, who was traveling in India. "He said, 'Don't worry about the mistakes. Most people get so caught up in their mistakes they miss the equity of the experience. The important thing now is that you withdraw the equity and invest it in the next endeavor.' "

Jason then flew home to spend time with his mom, sister, and a few close friends. There was a common thread amidst the abundance of advice: all reminded him of the courage that led him to quit a six-figure job at twenty-two years old. The reminder proved to be the final boost.

"While it's never exactly *easy* to venture out again," Jason explained, "it has become somewhat of a sick thrill for me. I tend to thrive off new opportunities to create something from scratch—"

What was his tipping point?

"I finally realized I was banking on stability when it wasn't that important to me. So my decision ultimately came down to whether I wanted to stick with an okay job for the chance my brainchild might walk. The financial implications could have been huge if it happened, but what if it took another two years? My biggest lesson came when I realized what I wanted most was to work at something I was passionate about. When I realized that, I stopped worrying about job stability and started figuring out how I could make money doing something I loved."

The difference-maker was Jason coming to terms with his higher need. Stability was important to him but not nearly as valuable as working toward something emotionally rewarding—something that ignited those warm fuzzies he spoke of.

Still, his circumstances would not have been so ideal for another job shift if the other offer from his brother and best friend had not come his way. This raises an important question: when our mind-set moves from the wrong need to the right one, do opportunities become more visible? Jason would say yes. "I had other opportunities come along over the past year, but I was so focused on making my situation [in the East] work out, that I didn't give them much thought . . . Now I have my best friend and my brother asking me for help in their ventures. And now I know why those offers excite me far more than a six-figure job I'm not that in to . . . The way I see it, there is risk either way. I'm just deciding I'd rather take a risk by forgoing stability instead of enjoyment."

Moving Toward Requirement/Reward Harmony

The truth is all jobs require tasks we don't love. Even dream jobs require mundane to-dos. Once you determine which job best suits you right now, the question you should ask at least twice a year is: Are my work requirements achieving the reward (or highest need) I seek?

If your highest need is currently stability via a comfortable job, then regularly ask the question this way: Are my work requirements achieving stability?

If your highest need is currently gratifying achievement via an inspirational job, then regularly ask the question this way: Are my work requirements achieving emotional gratification?

Jason's requirement/reward tension began turning toward harmony when he moved toward work requirements that allowed him to consistently achieve his higher need. To do the same, you must make two activities the core of your work ethic. The combination will arm you with the resources for harmonizing any requirement/reward tension that arises.

Activity #1: Habitual Excellence

The person committed to doing every task with excellence achieves more than a personal pat on the back. Habitual excellence opens doors whether or not it is recognized in the context of your particular organization.

Habitual excellence increases self-knowledge. Because Jason remained committed to doing great work at the larger company's headquarters—despite its uninspiring requirements—he gained invaluable self-knowledge that propelled him to a high level of confidence for his future endeavors. If you carry out only rewarding tasks with excellence, you will learn nothing new about yourself. And who's to say you have already discovered your greatest strength or highest joy? The process of finding your requirement/reward harmony will always coincide with an earnest process of self-discovery. That requires studying what you do and do not prefer, and your level of confidence with the former has much to do with your experience with the latter.

Habitual excellence builds momentum. Landing the perfect job does not mean you will always have perfectly scripted days full of perfectly suited tasks. Work will still feel like work at times, but it's in those moments that your character is forged. If your character withstands the test of mundane tasks, you will be equipped to exploit great opportunities. In most cases, the inability to capitalize on an opportunity is a momentum issue, not a recognition issue. Many see opportunities but are ill-equipped to seize them in their ripest hour because they lack momentum of character. They might try to close the preparation gap quickly, but by the time they are ready, the opportunity has usually passed. Habitual excellence ensures you always have momentum to jump after opportunities at the perfect time.

Habitual excellence builds strong alliances for future endeavors. Despite his eventual move back West, Jason's commitment to excellence earned him a high level of respect at the larger firm. Although the key players hated to see him move on, their respect for Jason compelled them to offer their resources for his next endeavor.

Activity #2: Full Engagement

The best way to earn equity in an experience is full engagement. A missionary named Jim Elliot said it this way: "Wherever you are, be all there." By being all there at your job, whether or not it's a perfect fit, you are placing deposits into your bank of experience that can be withdrawn now or down the road. When Jason sat down at his stepfather's suggestion and figured up the equity he'd earned in the East Coast experience, he'd obviously gained a ton of knowledge about the insurance industry. He initially downplayed it until he realized his industry knowledge included unique insight into its shortcomings—namely, the unfavorable reputation of insurance brokers and the lack of disclosure surrounding commissions. While selling insurance didn't excite Jason, improving the face of an industry did.

Once back West, he hammered out an idea in the evenings while helping his best friend and his brother with their ventures during the day. Soon the spark of an idea caught wind. Today that idea, Ensure Charity, is spreading like wildfire. Its business model has forever changed the life insurance landscape. It is the first brokerage in the history of the industry to donate half of each commission to the charity of the client's choice. The model is overtly generous, but it is also genius. The commission rate in the insurance industry is standardized and cannot be reduced to lure clients. With Ensure Charity, Jason reduced the "perceived cost" of commission. By using his firm, clients are paying for services, yes. But they are simultaneously changing lives by financially supporting causes they believe in.

Maintaining Requirements/Rewards Harmony

Is there a perfect formula for maintaining a work/life harmony where requirements consistently promote rewards? Yes. It's called keeping your circumstances in check so the effect of your job requirements remains rewarding. In other words, it meets your higher need. This is nothing groundbreaking, but it's something the vast majority doesn't do.

If we separated the American workforce into groups based on job alignment or how fully their jobs align with their higher-life need (stability or gratification), statistics would continually indicate the following.

- The biggest group (35–45%) would be misaligned and unhappy. I call this group *dysfunctional*.
- The middle group (25–35%) would be partially aligned and compliant. I call this group *functional*.
- The smallest group (10–20%) would be fully aligned and passionate. I call this group *superfunctional*.

Getting to the middle group would be a big step for most. If you've determined your circumstances are disheartening, make it your first goal to move from a dysfunctional to a functional place. To do so, practice habitual excellence, full engagement, and take the following two steps:

1. *Invest in personal growth.* Most people in the dysfunctional group remain there because they lack self-knowledge. They know they're unhappy, but they don't know what else to do. To move to the middle group, get to know your strengths so options for better harmony will become clearer. Marcus Buckingham's strengths test is an excellent resource for this (www.marcusbuckingham.com).
2. *Let others evaluate your circumstances.* Many people in the dysfunctional group have an unrealistic or inaccurate notion of their circumstances. Allowing others you trust to give an objective assessment of your job requirements

and objectives will bring your situation into focus. In many cases, a small change in perspective or attitude can make a big difference. Building Champions (www.buildingchampions.com) has a strong track record of helping business professionals assess their strengths and opportunities.

If you're like Jason, grateful for your job but not necessarily invigorated by it, you're in the middle group. There is nothing wrong with remaining in the middle group, especially if your higher need is currently stability. The truth is, you can live a very good life with a functional career. Some of my dearest friends do excellent, fully engaged work forty hours a week and have wonderfully full lives outside their jobs. They sustain energy and contentment by promoting their life values around a predictable work schedule and salary. There's no arguing with that strategy.

There is also no arguing with those who take it one step further. If, like Jason, you long for more from life than what you can experience away from the job, your best option is work circumstances for which you are passionate—a work/life continuum that is gratifying all your waking hours.

Moving from the functional group to the superfunctional group is the biggest step, but it is also the most rewarding. The potential is for fully aligned days where what is required of you consistently produces what is most rewarding for you. That brings me back to Maslow's pyramid of needs.

In the end, I believe Maslow's assessment of the highest human need holds true. While our pyramids may not all ascend in the way he suggested, I am certain that at the top of every person's pyramid is the need for what Maslow called self-actualization. It's that superfunctional place where you are investing the best of yourself into everyday activities. It is also the place of greatest requirement/reward harmony. While your circumstances might not make it your next logical destination, I encourage you to make the superfunctional group your ultimate destination.

> We are at our very best, and we are happiest, when we are fully engaged in work we enjoy on the journey toward the goal we've established for ourselves. It gives meaning to our time off and comfort to our sleep. It makes everything else in life so wonderful, so worthwhile.
>
> —Earl Nightengale

Making Money vs. Making Memories

> In March of 2002, I hit a point of high tension. If I stayed at work, I
> was missing family time; if I went home, I was losing ground in my
> business. Either way, I was leaving something on the table.
>
> —Sonny

O f all points of tension, the most common is the one that exists between your need to produce income and your need to engage in meaningful relationships. This tension is often the most pronounced sign that your circumstances are not as harmonious as you'd like. By the time a Texan named Sonny acknowledged his struggle with it, everything important had been stretched to a breaking point.

By 1998, when the Austin real estate market and his own career goals were primed for red-hot expansion, Sonny had already been a star performer at a national mortgage company for eight years. Setting his sights still higher, he bought a branch of the company himself and ran it solo until a lucrative refinance boom inspired him to recruit a partner. The move was perfectly timed, and the business exploded overnight. Sonny quickly hired more employees to stay ahead of the flood of business and worked long days to net all the money he could.

Four years later, Sonny's firm was averaging $100 million a year in mortgages and clearing $10 million in annual revenue. It was more

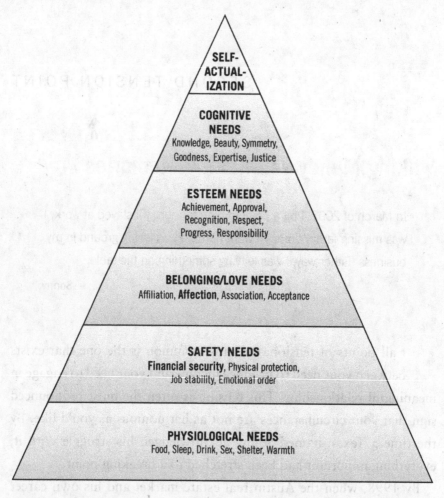

SELF-ACTUAL-IZATION

COGNITIVE NEEDS
Knowledge, Beauty, Symmetry,
Goodness, Expertise, Justice

ESTEEM NEEDS
Achievement, Approval,
Recognition, Respect,
Progress, Responsibility

BELONGING/LOVE NEEDS
Affiliation, **Affection**, Association, Acceptance

SAFETY NEEDS
Financial security, Physical protection,
Job stability, Emotional order

PHYSIOLOGICAL NEEDS
Food, Sleep, Drink, Sex, Shelter, Warmth

An adequate, stable income is an essential part of a secure life. But how do you balance the drive to produce with your natural need for personal relationships?

money than he had ever dreamed possible, and he was rightfully proud of his accomplishment. Unfortunately, the success had come at a significant yet totally unforeseen cost.

The Breaking Point

One night during his firm's fifth year, Sonny returned home typically late to find his wife, Carla, and their one-year-old son already asleep as usual. Tiptoeing through the bedroom, he noticed an object propped up on the dresser. He let his eyes adjust to the dark and then leaned in. It was a note with his name handwritten on the outside. He picked it up, slipped into the master closet, and turned on the light.

As he read what his wife had written, the words hit him like a brick across the jaw. "I don't want our children to grow up with a dad who comes home from work so angry and stressed they're afraid to play with him. The only time I ever see you it's the back of your head as you're leaving or the back of your head as you're lying down."

Sonny felt his blood starting to boil. *If she wants the big house and the ability to stay home with the kids every day,* he muttered to himself, *then Daddy's got to work, and it's not always gonna be pretty.*

Fortunately, Sonny didn't act on his first emotion. He paused, reread the note, and this time her words opened him up. He sat down on the closet floor and began to cry.

"It was a long and painful night," he confessed. "I knew she was right. I'd go three or four days without seeing my one-year-old son. Sometimes, if he didn't wake up in the middle of the night, I wouldn't see him for a week. I'd also been promising her for years that I'd be home for dinner and had yet to follow through. As I sat there in tears, I suddenly realized that I was just as concerned as she was. I was headed for destruction, and I was nowhere near the man I wanted to be."

That night Sonny vowed to make things better. "But," he admitted, "I had no clue how."

The Fork in the Road to Harmony

The problem with life, as the saying goes, is that it's daily. In other words, most of us reach a point where life will no longer slow down on its own. Taking a breather and evaluating—truly assessing—your circumstances requires a significant effort. Instead of putting forth that effort, many put up blinders and maintain speed—until a note shows up on the dresser in the middle of the night.

There are many theories about why people don't directly address their tension between making money and making memories, but one factor for certain is fear. We know that improving will require sacrifice, and we fear what that might mean: loss of financial stability if we cut back on work and loss of relational security if we cut back on free time.

The truth in hindsight, however, is that the loss is rarely as bad as we imagined, and the gain far better than we anticipated. Sonny would agree with that now. But at the time, taking steps toward harmony took immense courage because he couldn't see the right path. This is often the case.

Making the transition from haphazard to harmonious days is undoubtedly tough, but the longer you ignore your tension the tougher it gets—especially at the particular point between money and memories. Because so much is at stake on either side, the unaddressed tension seeps deeper and deeper beneath the surface until it begins to permeate other areas of life.

"My main problem," admitted Sonny, "was that I had a way of justifying everything—the late hours, the missed dinners, the postponed vacations—all as part of being successful. All the while I was angry, but I never took the time to understand where my anger was coming from. I was detached from reality, so I justified my busyness as a necessary evil."

In addition to detaching from the tension, Sonny ignored some deep-seated issues in his business. "Because we tried to capture all the business we could," he explained, "we grew without DNA, like a tumor. There was a lot of chaos, no systems, no vision, and no filter for who we were hiring. I looked at it like, 'Growth is growth and growth is good.' It was a painful existence but a dull pain—like boiling a frog—so I didn't feel what was happening until I was four years into it."

Perhaps you can relate. And perhaps it is difficult for you to foresee transitioning from your current chaos to harmony. Sonny was no different, but today he can offer some hindsight wisdom.

"I think one of the big hindrances to change is success," he said. "It is hard to make changes when you're already successful and you got there with the wrong people or the wrong systems. When I shared my new plans [to make changes] with some close friends, they said, 'You're crazy. You'll never be able to do it.' But I knew it was necessary. And when I see how my relationships are growing now and how well my business is thriving without all the stress and dysfunction, I don't question my decision for a second."

Safeguarding Your Path to Harmony

As you wrestle with the notion of making the changes necessary to harmonize your money/memories tension, there is an important preparation step that will help you over the hump of hesitancy, as well as two critical practices to put into action.

Your Preparation Step: Seek an Experienced Viewpoint

For Sonny to acknowledge his underlying tension was significant, but it wasn't significant progress. It was a confession but not a resolution. Too often people will see a problem, even acknowledge the tension to the point they can describe its precise effects, but then go no further. And acknowledgement without action can make matters even worse.

Sonny took the effect of his tension seriously. He knew it would eventually end in ill-health, parental dysfunction, and divorce. Still, he was unsure what to do because he couldn't just quit working and put his family in dire straights. Desperate and determined, he phoned an old fishing buddy.

"Tom was a friend who had changed," Sonny remembered. "We used to take fishing trips off the coast and talk about this kind of stuff. I'd tell him, 'Well, you get to walk on water, but the rest of us have to learn how to swim.' He made everything look easy—very efficient and successful on the job; very happy off the job. I called him and told him I needed to talk. We went to breakfast a few days later, and I was honest."

When suffering through the turmoil of money/memories tension, it's only logical to seek an experienced viewpoint. This is precisely what you should do before making any adjustments. Unfortunately, most don't—less than one-quarter of us, if you recall the statistic from the last chapter. There are three main reasons for this:

1. We glorify the tension.
2. We are not convinced of the negative effects.
3. We are embarrassed.

The first is the most common and springs from the perception that being too busy is a status symbol. Busyness falsly assumes we are successful and popular and in high demand. The problem with building your life on the foundation of a perception is that it's only a paper façade. It won't stand up to the storms of life. When Sonny's wife dropped the bomb, his walls caved in, and he was forced to live amidst the ruin or rebuild.

I assume that since you picked up this book you don't buy into the second notion that you are unaffected by your money/memories tension. While it's true that you might not always feel the negative effects or see the evidence, it's only a matter of time before it boils to the surface and you must address it or be called a fool. Sonny had a choice once the effects he'd been ignoring were illuminated. Fortunately, he didn't hide his eyes. Neither should you.

If you're falling prey to embarrassment, you are in good company. Everyone feels some humiliation from the act of backtracking, but it's far better than procrastinating for so long that recovery is no longer possible. Sonny was near the point of no return before Tom's viewpoint gave him inspiration and hope.

Over breakfast Tom plainly laid it out. "He told me there was no quick fix," Sonny recalled. "Because I had built my business with so much dysfunction, he said I would have to make some major changes. It was simultaneously what I didn't want to hear and what I knew I needed to hear. But I trusted Tom. He knew me and knew I loved my family and also loved what I did for a living. His directness helped me see that what I needed to accomplish was not going to be easy, but it was absolutely possible. His words also assured me it would be very worth it. He gave me hope because I knew he'd done it himself."

Let's be honest; change is difficult, whether it's getting up an hour earlier or eating two hours later or something more radical like shortening your workday. Before launching into some necessary, harmony-promoting changes, get some support. Like Sonny, you may find that many people think "it won't work." But those who know your heart will want the best for you. They will give you needed objectivity and encouragement—both key ingredients not only for making your necessary changes toward harmony but also for sustaining them.

The Two Key Practices You Must Adopt

When you and your supporters have defined what it'll take to bring more harmony to your days, don't hesitate. Changing won't get easier with time. After Sonny's breakfast with Tom, he knew he needed to move while he still had the guts to do it. To pull the changes off, Sonny adopted two daily practices that above all others represent the "how-to" of transitioning from money/memories tension to money/memories harmony. While your situation might differ from Sonny's and require some specific actions that aren't covered here, it is highly likely that by adopting the following two practices, you will immediately begin to see more harmony in your days.

Daily Practice #1: Manufacture Memories

To make money and memories simultaneously, you must be ready for unplanned moments of magic. The most significant event of your day will rarely be something you've put on a schedule. If you're myopic or perpetually caught up in the current of checklists, you risk passing off memory-making opportunities as interruptions.

Author Tim Sanders explained that memories fall in two categories:

1. Ones that occur as a natural by-product of healthy relationships.
2. Ones that occur as a manufactured by-product of intention.[1]

Because your various, instinctive needs are perpetually competing among themselves for your time, you will often find yourself in a season where naturally occurring memories (the first category) are few and far between. Whether it is a big opportunity at work or a personal difficulty that requires all your attention, in such one-sided seasons you must learn the art of manufacturing memories in order to keep your days harmonious. The best way to do this is to filter daily interruptions through your personal value-funnel. Here's what that means in my life.

Recently I was working hard at my office on an important project, when my wife dropped off my two boys. I greeted them with hugs and then returned to my desk to stick with the plan: the boys tapping away at their video game for a couple of hours and me staying focused on my work. But as my boys claimed the bay window chairs and started playing, I glanced past them to the ocean below and had a wild thought. "Guys," I said to them, "who wants to go snorkeling?"

They tossed their controls to the ground and fifteen minutes later the three of us were snorkeling in the cove with rented gear. We spent the next hour circling and splashing and sharing our underwater discoveries, and it was all something very manufactured and very memorable. I was not planning to get wet that afternoon. I was focused on doing my job and making money for my family. My boys were planning on some gaming time at their dad's office. But what memories would come from that scenario? Probably none. So instead, I allowed an interruption to produce something vastly more meaningful than one more hour of work. I manufactured a memory that would not have existed otherwise, and I made up the work later that week.

Your life has seasons in which you must be intentional about creating memories if you're to have any memories at all. The natural responsibilities of work and life will often pull you toward a memory-less routine. Clocking in and clocking out at work. Checking in and checking out at home. While routine and focus have their places, all your days must at the very least have room for manufactured memories. Adopting this practice will ensure that those days cultivate money/memories harmony, no matter how busy or focused you become. Here's a quick checklist to help you determine when the opportunity is right to manufacture a memory:

1. Can I live with the sacrifice I will need to make?
2. Is the individual (or individuals) worth my sacrifice?
3. If I say no to the opportunity, might I be sorry?

If you can answer yes to two of the three questions, the opportunity before you is ideal for a manufactured memory.

Daily Practice #2: Fight for Flexibility

Speaking of getting wet, what gave the three snorkelers in the introduction the option to set their own schedules was more than good luck. They did one of three things to maintain enough control to ensure harmony:

1. *They took a job with flexibility built in.* The event planner took the ideal route, but one that takes due diligence. Before accepting a position that appears on paper to have flexibility built in, talk to your direct report about expectations. You must make sure your version of flexibility and the company's version line up. Be reasonable, and don't expect more than what is perceived from the job description and what you've been told about the position.

2. *They negotiated for flexibility.* The mortgage professional replaced an overwhelming boss with one who understood what mattered most was overall productivity, not total hours worked. Today's marketplace is more adaptable than ever, so don't be afraid to ask—and don't think you have to seek another job. If a company already sees value in you, it will often be willing to bend the rules if you can prove it won't affect your performance or company morale. To offer proof, make yourself accountable. Offer more frequent productivity reports than the norm. Or even go so far as to put your job on the line if you don't perform up to standards over a given period of time (say between one and six months, depending on the situation). If affecting company morale—that is, "Others won't think it is fair"—is the hurdle, offer to take your case to the coworkers it might affect and receive their permission. Not everyone wants flexible hours, and most won't care what you do. But if it turns out that others want the same flexibility as you're seeking, negotiate the same accountability arrangement for all of you.

3. *They earned flexibility by consistent performance* (the waiter). This is obviously the surest way to achieve flexibility on the job. To ensure your hard work pays off in this way, talk to your direct report up front and ask for a time line in which you will prove your value to the company and at the end of which you will receive a measure of flexibility in your schedule—perhaps three days in the office and two days out of the office. If you've already proven yourself to your company for at least a year, you might be able to shorten the time line to more flexibility. If you've proven yourself for more than three years, it's very likely that your direct report will allow an immediate measure of flexibility. If you take this option, the strength of your case lies in your consistent performance, whether it comes before you ask or after.

Your Ultimate Motivation

When it comes down to achieving money/memories harmony, you must have a strong enough reason to follow through with the necessary changes, especially because they usually take a big effort.

Great reasons to go after money/memories harmony:

1. To improve your health
2. To have more time for favorite pastimes
3. To have more time for family and friends
4. To be more inspired, creative, and productive on the job
5. To be more passionate about everyday life
6. To take better care of your children

When Sonny set out to manufacture memories and fight for flexibility, he realized the truth of Tom's words. He faced a mountain to climb, and the only thing that would keep him going was his love for his family and a strong desire to build a lasting foundation for his business. He knew the latter would allow him to be very good at the former and ultimately become the man he envisioned himself being. He would give it his best effort, and Carla would be his greatest supporter.

"I told her I needed to work hard for three months without a day off," Sonny said. "I told her I would work late and it would be more sacrifice for our family, but in the end, after the three months, I would come home every night at 6:00 p.m., we would have one date night a week and one night a week dedicated to family, and I would schedule time for regular exercise and a good diet. She was inspired by it—and I went berserk for ninety days."

Because he was his own boss, making changes was not as easy as making new commitments and talking to a superior. Whatever he decided to do ultimately affected his employees, and it didn't take long for him to see that not everyone was on board with the new Sonny. "Massive struggles" is how he described his initial transition at work. "I realized that I was trying to bring everyone with me, and not everyone wanted to go. Not everyone wanted the same things I did."

Sonny paid a big price to achieve money/memories harmony. "I'm still paying for it today," he admitted. "We went from more than $100 million a year to $18 million. We had a six-figure loss on our P and L statement. We went from twenty-five to four employees in fourteen months . . . It was a horrible business decision but the best life decision I've ever made."

In the end, Sonny's business partner wanted out, but his core employees bought into his vision for the firm. He continued, "We shut down the office for three days and holed up in a hotel and talked about what we wanted from the business. We analyzed our core values, our relationships on and off the job, our big goals. We discovered that our group passion was building enduring relationships and caring for people more so than closing mortgages. So we created systems that allowed us to be productive but keep our core values at the top."

The Ultimate Effect of Money/Memories Harmony

What began to happen next is testimony to the sweeping effect of more harmonious days. "I was never a great producer," Sonny admitted, "but I still went from closing $10 million a year in loans to $40 million while keeping my commitment to get home at six every night. Actually, about halfway through the first year, I took my wife on a trip to celebrate the positive changes and she came home pregnant, so I got my bonus baby too."

The tough transitional days now past, Sonny can smile about his former self. "I've always wanted to write a book called *Sucksess,* and now I probably have all the material I need. I'm not anywhere near perfect at all of this, but I'm far better than I was, and now I'm surrounded by systems and people to support what I want to accomplish in a day. They also allow me to make choices and adjustments without major consequences."

We asked Sonny for the most important lesson from his experience, and his words foreshadow the long-term value of harmonizing your money/memories tension: "I learned that the most important things don't happen accidentally. Even though I've made some big financial sacrifices, over the next five to ten years I firmly believe I will find they were actually great investments instead of sacrifices. I am finally confident in the direction I'm going. Instead of constantly worrying about implosion, I finally know where my days will lead me.

"On our anniversary two years after the changes, I asked Carla, 'How do you like me now?' In reply she wrote an eight-page letter thanking me for everything that had happened." The letter gushed with affection and gratitude, its tone 180 degrees from the somber late-night note that started it all.

Sustaining Money/Memories Harmony

Knowing that efforts to manufacture memories and fight for flexibility are constantly tested, we ended our conversation with Sonny with a practical question: How do you continue on the same path today?

"Honestly," Sonny concluded, "I don't trust my own judgment because I am so passionate about my work. I can justify late hours. So I constantly go back and ask my wife how I'm doing. She is my gauge, and I've had to deal with some tough responses from her. But usually all she says is, 'I just don't understand why you're getting so stressed about everything.'" Sonny's wife acts as a teetering balance. When he leans too much toward the side of work, she helps bring him back to the center; a great picture of life on the wire.

Five years removed from that long and painful night in the closet, Sonny's response is refreshingly humble and enlightening. Most of all, it demonstrates the organic nature of money/memories tension—and how your reaction to it determines whether the result is harm or harmony.

When a friend calls to me from the road
And slows his horse to a meaning walk,
I don't stand still and look around
On all the hills I haven't hoed,
And shout from where I am, What is it?
No, not as there is a time to talk.
I thrust my hoe in the mellow ground,
Blade-end up and five feet tall,
And plod: I go up to the stone wall
For a friendly visit.

—Robert Frost

Taking Risks vs. Taking Responsibility

I started to realize that you can't just say, "Do what makes you happy." There is always something beyond what you're doing; always a bigger cause with bigger implications.

—Brad Martin

As he described his work ethic, Brad Martin confessed he "graduated on Sunday and started working on Monday." For nine years he kept the pace, holding seventy-, eighty-, and ninety-hour-a-week jobs, working his way from a small firm in Santa Barbara to the corporate office in Irvine and then to a bigger firm in downtown Los Angeles. Eventually he and his wife, Ana, settled in San Marcos, California, a northeastern suburb of San Diego, where Brad held a job as an equity analyst for a major hedge fund.

This would be the setting for a major life lesson.

At the time of their move to San Diego in 2002, Brad was earning enough money that the soaring cost of Southern California living was a fleeting thought. Ana took a job as a Spanish teacher at a nearby high school, and the couple banked her entire paycheck.

"Living in San Diego was no problem with that job," he admitted. "Ana didn't need to work. We had no debt. We didn't have to think

35

about buying anything—the money was always there. We didn't live extravagantly, but we didn't have any worries either."

The tide first began to turn when Brad started moonlighting as a quarterback coach for the football team at Ana's school. "I was already being exposed to the school at different sporting events, dances, and banquets that we attended. I started to get to know one of the football coaches pretty well. Eventually, he asked me if I wanted to coach."

A former college quarterback, Brad was easily intrigued despite the money—an eighteen hundred dollar stipend for thirty hours a week over a four-month period.

"Obviously, it wasn't about the money," he explained. "It only came out to about four dollars an hour." If anything, it was a hobby, a gratifying diversion from the daily grind. He welcomed it.

When We Start to Notice

Despite adding to an already congested schedule, Brad was learning about himself through coaching. This is something that seems to happen whether or not we mean for it to. We step outside the walls of our normal routine, and suddenly we begin to see and feel things differently. The new sensations often remind us that there is more life to be lived outside our small existence. If you pay attention to these feelings, they can become a catalyst for better things just over the horizon.

Through coaching, Brad started building authentic relationships for, he admitted, "the first time in a long time. And I was part of the positive change happening in these players' lives."

It was a far more invigorating experience than his analyst position afforded him. "It was about more than just making rich people richer," as he put it. Eventually coaching became a wider lens through which Brad would begin viewing his life.

Through a series of subsequent conversations with friends and family, Brad got honest with himself.

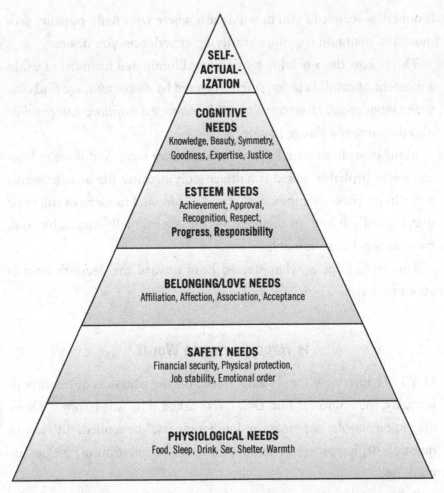

SELF-
ACTUAL-
IZATION

**COGNITIVE
NEEDS**
Knowledge, Beauty, Symmetry,
Goodness, Expertise, Justice

ESTEEM NEEDS
Achievement, Approval,
Recognition, Respect,
Progress, Responsibility

BELONGING/LOVE NEEDS
Affiliation, Affection, Association, Acceptance

SAFETY NEEDS
Financial security, Physical protection,
Job stability, Emotional order

PHYSIOLOGICAL NEEDS
Food, Sleep, Drink, Sex, Shelter, Warmth

Tension points may crop up anywhere on the pyramid, and esteem needs are often the most difficult to fulfill. The more you grow as a person, the more your responsibility will grow.

"I started to realize that you can't just say, 'Do what makes you happy.' There is always something beyond what you're doing; always a bigger cause with bigger implications."

When the greater cause of your work loses its luster, something often begins to tug at your insides. A series of questions begins to swirl in your head. It typically starts with, *Am I happy doing this?* and then evolves to, *What makes me happy?* and eventually arrives at, *What do I ultimately want from life?* The final question—if you dare to answer it honestly—can lead you down a path where your daily pursuits promote and maintain the more gratifying experiences you desire.

This is how the work/life tension gets illuminated for most of us. In a moment of candid clarity, often triggered by discontent, we find ourselves wondering, *How can I possibly manage a fulfilling career while also pursuing the things I value off the job?*

Many of us have posed that question before now. And if we're honest, we've probably asked it halfheartedly because the answer seems either improbable or impractical. Yet, deep down, I think most still hope that a good job and an invigorating life are mutually attainable and, more important, sustainable.

This same hope is what steered Brad toward the decision he was about to make.

Is *Happy* a Yuppie Word?

In a 1991 interview for *Rolling Stone,* on the occasion of his fiftieth birthday, the immortal Bob Dylan was asked if he was happy. "Those are yuppie words, happiness and unhappiness," he replied. "It's not [a question of] happiness or unhappiness, it's [a question of] blessed or unblessed."[1]

Bob's conclusion is similar to one that Brad was coming to as he considered his equity analyst position. While he could say he was doing something that made him happy—he enjoyed exercising his knack for numbers and the financial stability it brought—the job did not give him the same level of satisfaction that coaching high school football did, nor did it promote the life off the job that he and his wife wanted. Had his happiness merely been a yuppie definition of the word? He was ready to consider the possibility.

He began weighing the pros and cons of his job. This is something we tend to do on the heels of an inspiring diversion from routine, such as traveling to a foreign country or reviving a beloved pastime. He and Ana began to ping-pong a series of questions:

- What do we *really* need in life?
- What standards do we set to support those needs?
- Now, how do we live according to those standards?

Their answers illuminated a disconnection between Brad's current work situation and the standards for life he and his wife desired. They acknowledged this tension and then talked about what changes could be made to achieve better harmony. In short, they tried to figure out how he could continue employing his knack for fiscal sense while they experienced a more gratifying life.

Making the Tension Work

Brad had previously been invited to apply for an open accountant position at Ana's school. The invitation suddenly became more inviting. The couple talked it over and decided Brad should apply even though it was counterintuitive from a career standpoint.

"We had to accept that I was basically deciding to cut my salary in half. We're programmed to get paid *more* for each new job, and I was potentially opting to go in the other direction. I knew my coworkers wouldn't understand, but I didn't have a social life. I barely had time for my wife."

Shortly after submitting his application, Brad was offered the position. He took the risk and resigned from his job at the investment firm.

At the time of our interview, six months had passed since Brad's career adjustment. When asked how he thought it was going, he was frank about the potential pitfalls of his choice yet no less resolved to make it work.

"I do think, *When Ana is pregnant, what then?* We can't sustain this new life without her working.

"As an analyst, my job was to forecast. I was always looking ahead, always trying to predict the future. With our new situation, everything became short-term. We still have three months of savings and no debt, but we can't think beyond the next month or two. I don't know what will happen when we start a family, but I have a responsibility, and I'll take care of that when it happens."

Better Opportunities = Better Harmony

Brad's story shows how reducing the tension between professional progress and personal responsibility requires a commitment to continually assess and, when necessary, embrace the multidimensional opportunities before you.

It is not inertia that makes it possible to simultaneously fulfill personal responsibilities and pursue professional progress. It is your ability to continually make purposeful adjustments as significant opportunities and unforeseen circumstances arise. This might occasionally mean a major career shift—even a risky one—as it did for Brad, who had been leaning toward work progress too heavily.

Here are two skills that are key to making those adjustments successfully in your own life and career.

Skill #1:
Assess Current Opportunities, Pursue the Best Ones

As a happily-married, financially stable thirty-year-old with a new home in balmy San Diego, Brad Martin didn't seem to need a reevaluation of his life. Still, he couldn't deny the mounting tension between his personal and professional worlds. Finally he did something about it.

First, he took a closer look at the opportunities before him. He weighed their value, their immediate impact on his and Ana's current circumstances, and then made two immediate decisions to reduce the tension.

Thus far, Brad's path has required a minor and major shift: first, reviving an old pastime, and second, a job change. And he acknowledged that his path will likely require more shifts down the road. (He mentioned a desire to eventually go back to school.)

The skill—*to assess and, when appropriate, pursue new and different opportunities in life*—is one you must improve to harmonize your personal responsibilities and professional progress. Fortunately, according to studies, it's a skill Generations X and Y are very good at. Their predecessors, however, saw things differently. "Generations before them . . . valued tenure and career advancement," reported Anna Bahney in a *New York Times* article. "But this group (Gen X and Y) sees the chutes in the world as interesting as the ladders."

To demonstrate, Bahney detailed the inspiring actions of seven unconnected professionals between twenty-six and thirty-five years old who, like Brad, kept their options open in an effort to maintain a more harmonious life. What Bahney's seven professionals had in common was that they had all quit constricting jobs and waited for a time before pursuing other opportunities. Some took weeks off—others took months—to wander the globe or visit out-of-state friends and family in order to recalibrate themselves for a new start.

One example is Jesse Keller, who at age thirty-two left his job as a software engineer after ten years to pursue a very different kind of goal: visiting all fifty-eight national parks. According to Bahney, there was more than whim behind Keller's expedition.

"As the retirement age pushes further back," Keller explained, "and the finances for that time of life are less and less certain, it was almost unconscionable not to take advantage of the opportunity to travel now when I had the money and the health."

> "The trick," admitted Keller, "is finding a job that has the balance built in so that I don't have to go off on a grand adventure to recover from work."[2]

A New Definition

Stories like Brad's and Jesse's indicate that the definition—and therefore the pursuit—of work/life harmony has evolved from one generation to the next.

Most of our parents and grandparents sought predictable, sustainable routine—one company, one vocation, one location. Today most workers are far less single-minded. We regularly seek channels of higher gratification on and off the job, and we go with whatever combination of work responsibility and life enjoyment satisfies us best.

This doesn't mean you give up trying to land the ideal job that enables a wonderful life and stick with it forever. It means you should embrace a more flexible, opportunistic approach to your career instead of resigning yourself to circumstances that diminish work/life harmony. Rather than keeping an uninspiring job for thirty years no matter what, figure a way to bail out before you burn out, or pull the plug before you drown.

New Opportunities = New Adventures

So often life starts out as a great adventure and then somewhere along the way it becomes disenchanting. Part of that is accepting the reality that you have to work to live. To achieve a more wholly gratifying life—to recapture that spirit of adventure—you have to figure out how to restore the old sense of enchantment within your grown-up reality.

In assessing the job opportunity at Ana's school, which might bring that enchantment back, Brad enlisted the advice of several trusted friends. One was a close friend who is the lead singer of a major rock band. The friend wrestled with similar disharmony as a married man who was often on the road. After listening to Brad weigh the pros and cons of his own situation, the friend told him he'd be crazy to stay in his current job when a better opportunity was in front of them. He should grab it while he had the chance.

Brad also got solid counsel from a former Super Bowl MVP who was now the head coach of the high school football team. "He's had all the money and accolades," Brad explained. "Traveled everywhere, played all the best golf courses, seen all the best sights. I asked him what he learned from all that, and he said, 'It took me awhile to realize that none of it really matters.'"

If you find a great new opportunity but see that it will require a major shift—a move, a loss of income, a change of lifestyle—don't act on impulse. First, get advice from those your decision will impact most. Second, get advice from trustworthy friends who can offer a broader, unbiased perspective. If the advice affirms the adjustment, then you're ready to take action.

Skill #2: Embrace Current Blessings

Achieving purposeful imbalance at this tension point also depends on your willingness to set your own standards for success rather than letting culture define them for you.

The big lie, said Brad, is that all the "stuff"—the comforts, the distinction, the affluence of business success—is necessary for a harmonious life.

"Life is kind of funny in that you'll find that stuff in other things, other opportunities. I've played Pebble Beach three times for business related things, but I would rather play golf with my brother or a close friend anywhere—on a public course even. In nine years I traveled everywhere, but I would rather travel down the street with Ana."

> Brad is learning the second skill for harmonizing this point of tension.
>
> We've seen that first of all you must regularly assess the opportunities before you and make shifts when and where necessary. Second, *you must develop a keen sense for perceiving and embracing the blessings before you now.*
>
> Side by side, these two skills can seem like a "one foot in the present, one foot in the future" approach. But, in fact, they're perfectly complementary.

Setting Personal Standards

You are defining your version of success when you answer the question, *What do I really want from life?* When your definition is clear, you can then apply the same standard to every opportunity, sifting each through the same funnel.

On the flip side, if you don't define success, it becomes a moving target that leads to a never-ending game of one-upmanship against yourself. You lack feelings of stability because your feet and focus are in the future—you're convinced that there's something better up ahead somewhere. This is a harmless tendency in itself, but, when magnified, it can keep you from embracing the good right in front of you. As a result, you not only devalue your current circumstances, but you also fail to distinguish a good opportunity from a bad one because it's not where you expect it to be.

You'll never achieve work/life harmony until you learn to appreciate the positives in what you already have. And you have to know what you have in order to realize what you still want and need.

Take an Honest Inventory

You can usually trace the struggle between personal responsibilities and professional progress back to a flaw in your thinking. You are thinking in the wrong direction if you are continually asking, *What am I missing today?* The question you should be asking instead is, *What is important to me today?* The most significant things in your life are the people and opportunities before you right now, because the future is not guaranteed. The only things you can be sure of are the things you can hold in your hand today, and what you do with them determines how successful you can be tomorrow.

You can't pursue purposeful imbalance within this point of tension from a scarcity mind-set: "I don't have this and that." If you do, you overlook all the joys, opportunities, adventures, and surprises of the present—essential ingredients for a harmonious existence. As long as you cling to a scarcity mind-set, neither work nor life will ever feel like enough.

To achieve a purposefully imbalanced approach, exchange that scarcity mind-set for an abundance mind-set: "I already have this and that." Instead of incessantly looking for the more, better, or different of tomorrow, learn to embrace the good of now. This doesn't mean you will find all the ingredients for better harmony directly in front of you, but it does mean you won't overlook the ingredients you already have. With time, it will become clear to you what you can and cannot live without. From that vantage point you can reliably make right decisions about whatever opportunities arise, allowing you to fill the harmony gaps between your personal responsibilities and professional progress. From there you can transition to a place of managing purposeful imbalance rather than fighting disharmony.

What Are We Fishing For?

Brad shared a memorable story with colleagues and friends that demonstrates the importance of evaluating current circumstances and making good choices as opportunities arise:

An American investment banker stood on the pier of a quaint Mexican village as a fisherman eased a small, wooden boat to the dock. The banker looked into the boat and noticed several large yellowfin tuna. He complimented the Mexican fisherman on the quality of his fish.

"How long did it take you to catch them?" he asked.

"Only a little while," replied the fisherman.

"Why didn't you stay out longer and catch more fish?" the banker asked.

"With these I have more than enough to meet my family's needs," replied the fisherman.

"But what do you do with the rest of your days?"

The fisherman thought for a moment, then replied: "I sleep late, fish a little, play with my children, take a siesta with my wife, and then stroll into the village each evening where I sip wine and play guitar with my amigos. I have a full life."

The American laughed. "I have a Harvard MBA and can help you be more successful. You should spend more time fishing and sell the fish your family doesn't need. With the money you could buy a bigger boat and hire other fisherman to bring in more fish. Eventually, with your profits, you could buy several boats so that you could send out a fleet every morning and bring home hundreds of fish to sell. Then, instead of selling your catch to a middleman, you would sell directly to the processor, eventually opening your own cannery. You would control your product, processing, and distribution. This would allow you to expand to other major markets like Mexico City, Los Angeles, Miami, and Manhattan. You would have an enormous enterprise!"

"But, how long would this take?" asked the fisherman.

"Ten to fifteen years," replied the banker.

"And then what?" asked the fisherman.

The banker giggled. "That's the best part—at just the right time, you would announce an IPO and sell your company stock to the public and become extremely rich. You would make millions!"

"Millions?" repeated the fisherman. "And then what?"

The banker thought for a moment. "I suppose you would retire to a small village on the coast where you could sleep late, fish when you wanted, spend time with your family, take afternoon naps with your wife, and spend evenings sipping wine and playing guitar with your amigos."

Seeing What We Already Have

The ability to take honest inventory of your life does not come naturally, but it's something you learn as you grow older. "You start out thinking that you're going to conquer the world," explained Andrew Oswald, a professor of economics at the University of Warwick in England. "Then you discover that it's tough out there and become dissatisfied. Happiness levels tend to bottom out around thirty. Eventually, after five or ten years, you come to terms with yourself. You learn to control your aspirations. After you've done that, it's easier to get steadily happier again."[3]

How can you immediately feel the benefits of a more harmonious life at this tension point between personal fulfillment and professional success? Brad has the answer but admitted it took a while to find it.

"Thinking about our situation used to make me crazy, stress me out," Brad explained. "But I realized we can pay the bills *now*. We have a great life *now*. If things change, we'll make changes and make it work. I'll get another job if I have to. I'll work to provide what my family needs. Ana and I were both raised without much money and we are fine."

He offered the voice of experience to everybody out there who's wrestling with the cost of making adjustments. "Staying in an awful situation in the name of responsibility is dangerous," Brad asserted. "It may be responsible to your bank account, but is it responsible to yourself? To your relationships?"

He went on to explain that for him right now, training his responsibility/progress tension toward harmony means consistently assessing and pursuing worthwhile opportunities to be: (1) a loving husband, (2) an excellent money manager, (3) a dependable friend, and (4) an inspiring coach. Since quitting his high-paying job, he has become open to any arrangement that synthesizes these four pursuits.

Embracing his outlook may give you a clearer picture of how to begin your own journey toward a harmonious life.

A Philosopher's Advice

Legend has it that Alexander the Great paid the Greek philosopher Diogenes a visit. As the two were exchanging final farewells, Diogenes asked Alexander if he had any plans. Alexander answered that he planned to conquer Greece. "Then what?" Diogenes asked. Alexander said he planned to conquer all of Asia Minor. "And then?" Alexander said he planned to conquer the world.

Diogenes persisted with his line of inquiry: "What next?" Alexander insisted that after conquering the world, he planned to relax and enjoy himself. Diogenes replied, "Why not save yourself a lot of trouble by relaxing and enjoying yourself now?"

It's a great question to ask yourself, especially now that you have the tools to answer it correctly.

Moving Up vs. Moving On

No matter what, your body doesn't want to stay on the high wire . . .
it wants to jump off to a place that's easier and safer. But what
progress is there in that?

—Matt Simms

Within each of us is a unique combination of skill and desire that bends us toward a particular life path. Some find their stride early on, but the majority of us have to plod and prod through peaks and valleys first. Still, the notion of a dream job has never seemed more possible. America is historically the land of opportunity, and the rules of the new working class are geared toward forging the right path early—before a family, a hefty mortgage, and/or other midlife factors make it more risky and complicated.

Yet the new rules are not all roses. For starters, too much career mobility looks bad on the résumé. It can imply unreliability and a lack of commitment to employers looking to invest in employees long-term. Furthermore, while company lifers are less common these days, there is something to be said for loyalty and the lessons that accompany tenure. There are certain character qualities you can't develop in short spurts.

On the other hand, the wherewithal to seize opportunities in their prime is invaluable. Those who are unable or unwilling to seize opportunity will likely find themselves on a career death-march down a dead-end street.

Somewhere amidst the efforts to find our ideal life we stumble on a tension point between our need to keep moving up our current path and our need to keep moving on to bigger and better paths. It's a great tug-of-war between making tangible progress and reaching our potential.

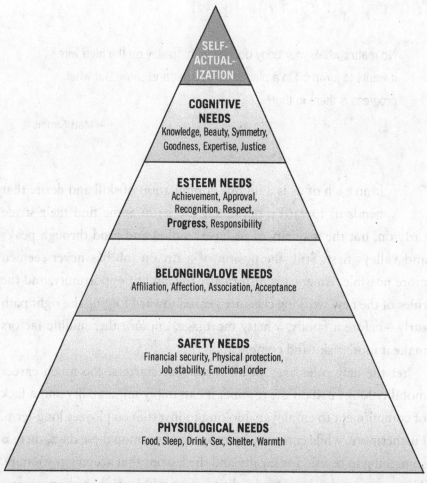

SELF-ACTUALIZATION

COGNITIVE NEEDS
Knowledge, Beauty, Symmetry, Goodness, Expertise, Justice

ESTEEM NEEDS
Achievement, Approval, Recognition, Respect, **Progress**, Responsibility

BELONGING/LOVE NEEDS
Affiliation, Affection, Association, Acceptance

SAFETY NEEDS
Financial security, Physical protection, Job stability, Emotional order

PHYSIOLOGICAL NEEDS
Food, Sleep, Drink, Sex, Shelter, Warmth

You cannot escape the need to keep making progress—to continue building whether on old familiar paths or promising new ones.

Matt Sims was a case in point. After graduating from college in 2000, he spent a year in Costa Rica, where amidst the lush landscape he began to think more seriously about his future. What path would he take? Where should it begin, and more important, where would it lead him?

Matt believed in a sense of calling, what some refer to as a life purpose. Yet he quickly discovered that establishing and following his life purpose wasn't as simple as regurgitating notes for a midterm exam. It eventually led him on a seven-year journey through a steep valley of self-evaluation and understanding. When we spoke, he was still sorting out the experience of the journey, which is why his thoughts on harmonizing the tension between moving up (progress) and moving on (potential) are so insightfully raw. They will serve us well as a guide to solving this all too common quandary.

Between Progress and Potential

The phrase "climbing the corporate ladder" became a mainstay during the late eighties but has since fallen from favor. It began to fade in the mid-nineties as Gen Xers (those now in their mid- to late-thirties) began wondering, *What if my ladder is leaning on the wrong building?* The more those workers thought about it, the more they doubted the value of whatever was at the top of their ladder and whether it would actually matter to them. Defying the protocol of previous generations, many stepped off their corporate ladders to start climbing new ones— presumably, the right ones.

As stories swirled around the watercooler of people who saved their souls by swapping ladders, the thought of spending twenty or thirty years at the same company seemed more and more senseless. Then around the turn of the twenty-first century, Gen Yers (most now in their mid- to late-twenties) begin entering the workforce with a general aversion to corporate ladders. A trend emerged: the younger the worker, the shorter the tenure. Before long, the prevailing career strategy leaned toward experimentation and short-term commitment—both aimed at finding the right ladder as early as possible.

When it was time for Matt to return to the States from his year in Costa Rica, a big decision loomed. "I figured it was easier to find a fulfilling job than an incredible wife," he explained. "I thought about joining the Marines but felt that Leighton [then his girlfriend] was a more rare opportunity . . . but getting married forced my hand with the job search."

In the months before his wedding, Matt tapped the resources of his alma mater for job openings that fit his logistics degree (a degree he admits was not his choice). His school came back with two good opportunities: one in Iowa and the other in Puerto Rico. With his recent immersion in Costa Rican culture and Leighton's good grasp of the Spanish language, the job in Puerto Rico seemed a perfect fit. One month after marrying, Matt and his bride moved to a suburb outside of San Juan to pursue a sales and marketing job with a major home improvement warehouser. It was the responsible decision given his recent marriage. Whether it was the right decision remained to be seen.

On the Rise and Moving Backward

Like most first jobs, this one had its pros and cons. One big pro was an immediate opportunity for Matt to showcase his strong work ethic and excellent people skills. A major con centered on the dog-eat-dog corporate climate. Trust was a buzzword but only sometimes a reality; the best worker wasn't always the most recognized worker.

"I learned a lot about the corporate world there," he explained. "I saw the typical ugly corporate stuff, and it drove me crazy—people sending out their big sales numbers to the entire company, constantly kissing the bosses' butts . . . My strategy was just to work hard and do a great job. I figured I'd be recognized better that way—the old fashioned way . . . [My strategy] helped me become a finalist for the big year-end award, but in the end the winner was the one who puckered the biggest and slapped his own back the loudest."

The experience soured Matt's taste for the corporate world. Looking back, he's not sure why he made his next decision but supposes the award incident had a lot to do with it.

As executives talked up a promotion he was offered during the weeks that followed, Matt caught a case of short-timer's disease. "I was grateful to be recognized as one of the finalists . . . but ultimately they began pushing me in a direction I didn't want to go. I began wondering what else was out there."

Like most, Matt's inclination was to keep moving up his current ladder. His employer was stable and his pay would only get better the higher he climbed. Yet his wanderlust eventually held sway. Despite the offer of a management position, Matt found himself revisiting the dreams he'd had in Costa Rica about more than a lucrative career— dreams about what he felt called to do with his life.

Voices from the Past

Faced with a decision either to move up his current ladder or on to a new opportunity, Matt's progress/potential tension rose. Accompanying the tension were some familiar but unfriendly voices, the loudest of which was his mother's. "Growing up, my mom always played the devil's advocate with me," Matt confessed. "As I got older and started talking about my dreams, she'd say things like, 'Dreams are fleeting, Matthew . . . You can't do that, Matthew . . . That's stupid, Matthew.' All of it was fear-based stuff—but at some point I started buying into it."

In the midst of his big decision, Matt began to realize his overzealous mother had hamstrung him. The more her message reverberated, the more hesitant he became.

As Matt pondered his options, he and Leighton took a weekend trip to Florida for her father's birthday. There, Matt's father-in-law offered him a sales job with his company. It was the most practical, mother-approved opportunity imaginable—and it would lead him in precisely the wrong direction. Matt is still working at that job and still complaining about it. He's stuck in the past, trying to meet an expectation his parents had laid down for him. His options are weakened by the worry of what tomorrow will hold and worry over the consequences of moving out from under the shadow of his past.

Here's a quote I love: "Worry does not empty tomorrow of its sorrow, it empties today of its strength." Never let fear guide your decisions. The only thing fear will do is diminish your mind-set for a present and future that must be predicated on strength of spirit and confidence.

"Looking back, I don't know why I even considered it," Matt said, "except that fear had a lot to do with it. I'd worked for [my father-in-law] before, in college over one summer, and it was a horrible experience . . . But I kept hearing my mom's voice and thinking, *It's a practical opportunity—close to home, in the same town as my in-laws . . . My dreams probably are unrealistic and stupid. I need to just suck it up and do this. There's a lot I can learn.*"

So often our inner self-speak springs from the voices of the past that have had significant impact on us. This is not always a bad thing, but it can be hobbling if it fills us with doubt. What voices from the past are speaking to you in your current circumstance? Are they negative or positive? Do they speak strength into your character or weakness into your soul? Release yourself from those voices haunting your present reality and move on. You're not letting go of a precious memory, you're scrubbing your mind and soul of a burr that can only hinder your personal and professional progress.

Although Matt accepted his father-in-law's offer with high expectations, his tension rose to a higher peak. When I spoke with him, two years had passed like ten. He was still toiling away for his father-in-law but actively searching for his next step. His voice was tired and heavy for a twenty-nine year old, yet still hinted at hope. The more we talked, the more the hope deep in his heart bubbled to the surface.

Risk and Reward

Unpleasant is a good word to describe Matt's experience, yet various studies indicate *common* might be more accurate. According to a 2005 *Men's Journal* study, approximately three-quarters of the American workforce are not in what they'd call dream jobs.[1] When Matt heard that statistic, he laughed and then confessed, "I'm actually surprised it's not higher." If his response echoes yours, it's likely you are also dealing with some progress/potential tension.

Matt is fortunate that his inner optimist dies hard. He has pushed through nearly a decade of indecision and mined some critical lessons that finally have him looking and leaning in the right direction. If you're struggling at this point of tension—floundering between your current ladder and a ladder with more potential—Matt's two primary lessons have something to teach you.

Lesson #1: Stay in the Tension

The most pressing step for harmonizing your progress/potential tension is counterintuitive. Everything in you might want to run from the tension to a place that's easy and predictable. But don't be fooled. More often than not, it's the worst thing you can do.

After a year in Florida working for his father-in-law, Matt was on the verge of breaking down. So he drove two hours to sit with a longtime friend in Orlando. While others—including a "bald-headed, round-glasses-wearing joke of a psychiatrist"—were telling him to just relax, his friend recommended something different. "He encouraged me to stay in the tension," Matt explained. "He said, 'Don't run from it. Stay in it and go after your dreams. It won't be easy, but if you stay in the tension, you'll be forced to figure it out.'"

It was a different voice from those he'd been fighting in his head. Most of all, it was a voice of hope—finally! "Things had gotten so bad," Matt admitted, "I was eating a ton and gaining weight. I was depressed and didn't want to get out of bed in the morning. I was just miserable . . . [My friend] helped me see it was okay to pursue my dreams. It wouldn't be easy, but it would be worth it in the long run."

If you're in the midst of rising progress/potential tension, resist the urge to get out right away. There is probably something important the tension can teach you about yourself and about a better path. Use what you learn to make a more harmonious next step—one that has you moving up the right ladder and on the right path.

Lesson #2: Risk Is Unavoidable

Matt's experience also illuminated another critical lesson: Risk is the unavoidable context of all true progress and potential. How you handle risk in your career is a major determinant of your level of work/life harmony. Below are the primary differences between those who handle risk well and those who don't. Which way do you lean with your decisions? Be honest.

Risk Taker	Risk Avoider
Pursues dreams	Placates dreams
Aspires for potential	Aspires for convenience

Calculates	Acts cautious or overcapricious
Thinks about progress	Thinks about pain
Pushes	Pleases
Shows resilience	Shows reluctance
Takes responsibility	Justifies decisions

Under the right conditions, every step up your current ladder will move you closer to your potential. To achieve full harmony at this point of tension always requires risk. For some this means forgoing a move up in order to move on to an opportunity with more potential. For others it means teetering on an uncertain ladder until they know enough to take a more harmonious next step.

The bottom line: when it comes to navigating the rungs of your career climb, it is a farce to think you can avoid risk altogether. While certain seasons of life call for the more practical choice, you have to choose with both progress and potential in mind. If not, the choice multiplies the risk. Matt learned that lesson after he chose to work for his father-in-law. If he'd calculated the risk of the choice, he now confesses he would have either turned it down or committed to it for only a short transition period. As it happened, he carelessly dove in headfirst, and it only caused more pain. That's the nature of risk: when you try to avoid it, you only increase it.

Calculating (and Taking) Your Steps to Harmony

Because Matt chose the practical option with his second job, he forced an even riskier choice that drove the level of progress/potential tension higher than ever: quit working for his father-in-law and invite family strife, or do nothing and remain miserable. To move up his current ladder was actually to regress. To move on was to invite more stress. It was a damned-if-you-do, damned-if-you-don't scenario. But it's what he had to work with, and he had to make a choice.

When you're at the peak of progress/potential tension, ignoring the decision will not help the situation. Making the safe or practical decision will likely make matters worse. The right decision is to step toward harmony. Here's how to know whether your best move is *upward* or *onward*. Signs that it is time to move *up* your current ladder are:

- Unsolicited affirmation from colleagues
- Superiors seem to need you more, or often seek your advice
- Interest from other employers in the same industry
- You like your company but aren't challenged in your position

Signs that it is time to move *on* to a ladder with more potential are:

- Declining enthusiasm
- Frequent clock-watching
- Regular daydreaming
- Job hunting on and off the job
- Depression

When Matt weighed the options to stay with his father-in-law's company or move on to something more fitting, it was obvious the greatest risk was in staying put. He needed to move on to a ladder with higher potential and then begin to move up again. Given his history, this was the last thing he felt capable of doing . . . but he knew it was precisely the step to take.

"The last seven years have been a lot like living with back pain," he said. "My parents left me with some pain, but I learned to walk around with it. Working for my father-in-law not only brought the pain back, it also made it worse. I could barely move. What I needed was the career version of a chiropractor. I needed someone to set me straight. Thankfully a friend finally did."

Matt asked Leighton for her advice about the conversation he knew he needed to have with her father. "She was very supportive and agreed that it needed to happen. She also helped me decide what should and should not be said. We both recognized the potential for family strife."

A week later, Matt initiated the dreaded conversation. He calls it a "stressful, sweaty experience" but one that went far better than expected. "He told me he understood and even encouraged me to keep working for him while I looked for my next job."

Though Matt didn't need the permission, his father-in-law's reaction fueled his search for a new ladder. The subsequent weeks revealed once again that moving toward progress/potential harmony is a worthwhile undertaking, but one that inevitably involves risk.

Since the conversation with his father-in-law, Matt has been making calls, giving interviews, and researching numerous options. As of this writing, nothing has changed on the surface—he still holds the same job. Beneath the surface, however, Matt is living in a new world. He's hopeful for the first time in longer than he can remember, and he is finally convinced that the shortest path to harmony is consistently linking his daily tasks to his dreams. This perspective is what he lacked all along to see which ladder was the right ladder for him.

"Good Enough" Never Is

It's tempting to freeze up and remain on the ladder you're on, buying into the notion that this is "as good as it gets." If you believe there's a unique path for your life, there can be no such thing. Being content with "as good as it gets" is the equivalent of admitting your progress has peaked and your potential is past. If it were actually true, there would be no reason for anyone ever to do anything but hang on to the status quo. No reason to dream, no reason to hope, no reason to meet anyone new or take on any new adventure. No reason to try.

This unfortunately is the way many people deal with progress/potential tension; they try to control it by dumbing down their dreams and lowering their expectations. Left to fester, those people become workplace cynics who ferret out gaps in every strategy and cracks in everyone's armor. If you need to know what's wrong with the world or the workplace, ask them, they'll know. It's all they think about.

The good news is that, all the while, their hearts go on beating so that if they're lucky they eventually see their cynical outpourings as manifestations of the frustration, disappointment, and fear they feel about themselves and their careers. What they need most is to feel the pit below the bottom step of the ladder they're on, where perspective is no longer subjective and the right ladder is their only need. This was the setting Matt described as the catalyst for his turnaround. "I think I had to get to the bottom," he said, "to see my situation for what it really was."

If you're in a pit now or merely sensing you need to move in a more purposeful direction, the question you should be answering is, *How do I move to a place where my daily progress pushes me toward my potential?*

It's easy to mindlessly ascend a corporate ladder without considering the impact each wrung will have on your potential. It's also easier to become a company lifer in the name of comfort than to seek out your strengths and listen to the longings of your heart. But the easier paths will never lead you to a dream fulfilled. Where do you really dream of going? What do you dream of achieving and experiencing in your lifetime? Now, what do you need to do to get there from here?

Matt's answer to those questions was unexpected, yet it reflected movement toward harmony at this point of tension. Think about how his answer compares with your own.

Daily Progress That Reaches Toward Potential

"I have spent the last seven years doing the safe and easy thing," Matt explained, "and while it almost killed me, it's also taught me what I need and don't need. In a way, it's forced me come up with my own definition of progress." His point is key to simultaneously moving up the right ladder and forward on the path to your potential.

What does progress mean to you? The lazy way to define it is to look around and borrow an advertiser's definition, your coworker's definition, or even your company's definition. Don't fall for those definitions. Though composing your own definition of progress is a straightforward process—once you remove what Matt calls "the false prophets of your future"—it requires a unique combination of honesty about the present and hope for the future.

Honesty about the present is the ability not to sugarcoat your current circumstances. Are you dissatisfied? Why specifically? What do you dislike most about your job? Why do you dislike it so much? If you're tasting something bitter, say so. Don't frost it and down it like a donut.

Now before your answers about the present can help you, you need outside input from trusted friends and colleagues. That's because your perspective is unavoidably subjective and therefore blind to certain factors. Matt, for instance, was blind to the fact that he was depressed because of the practical choices he had made. He saw them as sensible choices—and therefore good—when the reality was that they were fear-based attempts at pleasing other family members. His clouded perspective didn't clear up until his Orlando friend offered a different take—that Matt was digging his own grave by ignoring his desires, which turned out to be the most *im*practical path he could take.

With a more honest perspective on his present circumstances, Matt was finally able to discern the lessons of seven tough years and begin applying them to his daily steps. This is where hope for the future comes into play.

Hope for the future requires the clarity of perspective Matt finally found. Perhaps he was prone to dreaming but not doing when he was little, and that had something to do with why his parents bombarded him with hyperpractical messages. Maybe they got the same messages when they were young. Regardless of the source, Matt grew to believe his highest hope was to be sensible—and if it wasn't, he was being naïve. But once his Orlando friend helped him view his present circumstances more objectively, Matt began to perceive his future differently. His hopes were free to reach beyond the land of practicality to a place of heartfelt potential.

While responsibility for his wife and young child require a certain level of caution, Matt now feels free to think big and envision a future that motivates him to make progressive decisions today. "The mistake," he said, "is that so many people—myself included—are used to thinking you have to 'put in your time' before you can expect your days to be a reflection of who you are. The putting-in-your-time part is what gets everyone hung up. We think it means sensible, detached steps are just the price of getting to do what we're really made to do, when in reality that couldn't be further from the truth. To step toward our dreams is hard, but ironically it's ultimately the safest path."

I asked Matt to sum up his new approach to progress, given the hard lessons he's gleaned.

"I'm to the point where I don't need a lot of money," he said. "I haven't had it for almost a decade . . . but we're down to one car and obviously need some. So when my wife and I talk about our situation, she best sums up my approach to progress when she says, 'Just do something in the direction you want to go. Just make sure you're truly moving forward.' I know she's right—my daily and weekly decisions have to move me closer to my dreams if things are going to continually improve."

How do you ensure continual progress toward your potential? "A lot of it," said Matt, "is a willingness to trust your gut. I was raised to trust only the tangible future—those things I could reasonably deduce would happen—the lessons I'd learn or the experience I'd gain or the good marks on my résumé I'd get. Now I realize that what's more important is the unforeseeable stuff—the emotions associated with what I'll be doing and the direction I'll be heading. That stuff is what I always pushed aside . . . I suppose it eventually caught up with me."

Transitioning to Progress Toward Potential Harmony

Transitioning out of your tension to a place where you're making daily progress toward your potential is no overnight process. Most initial steps toward your potential are small, and it is only in their cumulative value that you see true progress. This can mean weeks and months of small, decisive steps without tangible confirmation that those steps are making a difference. You have to trust your gut and keep moving. Matt offered some insight on how to do this—how to, as he said, "remain patient and progressive at the same time."

"I think the patience comes from giving up more of myself—the parts that aren't necessary to get where I want to go. It's easier to be patient when you understand that realizing your potential requires becoming a certain person too. It's not all about getting to do certain things. I used to think I just had to figure out how to do the thing I was made to do. But I've realized I might not be prepared to do that yet . . . So I've learned that who I am becoming is as important as what I am doing—

"The simultaneous progressiveness comes from believing there is a greater purpose for me and never dumbing that down just to feel more accomplished. It also comes from believing that my purpose looks more like a path than a destination. So the reality is that I can realize my potential every day if I make purpose-minded decisions. Sure, my potential will look better a year from now—but I'm not there yet. I'm here, and I have decisions to make today that will allow me to tap into my current potential—and simultaneously make progress toward who I'll be and what I'll be doing a year from now."

We can break Matt's insight down into the two core activities he highlights:

- Becoming a better you
- Doing more purposeful work

By making these two tasks the umbrella over your daily to-do list, you will begin to transition into daily progress that moves you toward steadily higher potential. This is the harmonious combination Maslow called "self-actualization," the process of becoming the best *you* in order to do your best work. He dubbed it the highest need of every human, and I find it hard to argue this claim. I don't know a single person without some degree of ambition. Don't we all seem to have an innate longing for something more? Love, meaning, purpose; no matter how you describe it, we all feel pulled toward something bigger, better, or more meaningful. You might say we're all innately mobile; we are made to move. But toward what? This is the question we must answer every day in order to move from progress/potential tension to progress/potential harmony.

A few years ago, *Men's Journal* came out with a practical guide to answering this question in your own unique way. The advice mirrors some valuable insight offered in Jim Collins's classic *Good to Great* and ensures that your daily movement embodies the harmony of progress-toward-potential.

Here's how to pave a path for making daily progress toward your highest potential. It may take some time, as in Matt's case, but once that path is paved, your job becomes merely to stay on it. Follow these three steps:

1. *Figure out what in the world you can be your best at.* What task puts you most in your zone? What skill could you excel in if you took the time to develop it? Everyone has at least one to three skills with above average proficiency. What are yours? When developed, they are your greatest career assets.

2. *Figure out how to maximize your personal income while doing it.* How can you make your best skills profitable? Can you use them to increase your value in your current position? Or do you need to move on to another ladder that will exercise your skills on a more regular basis? While I believe everyone holds the seed of an entrepreneurial spirit, I don't believe everyone has to start a business, foundation, or movement to maximize the value of their best skills. With some focused research, the vast majority of us can find positions in reputable organizations that put our best skills in their zones. If you're not currently working for such an organization, you can still progress toward your potential by doing due diligence each week to find a better organization. The goal with this second step is to figure out how to make a living by using your best skills. It may take some time, but all steps in this direction are progress toward potential. Stay on track until you figure it out.

3. *Devise a plan to do it.* This step might require what Matt's parents would consider "impractical" decisions. For some it will mean taking a new job or at least transferring to a new department. If that's your situation, plan ahead for it. Don't make the mistake of quitting without having another opportunity ready to step into. That move will likely put you in a situation where you are pressed by time, and the longer you're without a job, the less selective you can be. Don't put yourself in that kind of pinch. Plan carefully for any job or career transition, even if the transition takes six months or longer, so that meeting your basic needs doesn't get in the way of meeting your higher needs.

Today Matt puts himself somewhere between Steps 1 and 2. And he's okay with that. It's still progress toward his potential. "I've learned so much about myself over the last few years," he says. "I have a good idea of what I can be great at, and now I'm in the process of figuring out how I can make a living using those skills . . . I'm figuring out what that process looks like—what the next step is. For instance, do I go back to school? Do I need some formal training before I can step into that position? Or will my education continue in my next job? Or can I find a job now that allows me to really use my best skills?

"Answering all the questions can still feel like a grind some days because I really just want to be doing the thing I'm made to do. It's especially hard when I see others in their dream jobs making good money. But I've learned to embrace my unique process and focus on who I am becoming and what I should be doing right now. I know there's always going to be some tension in that, but the difference between the tension I feel now and the tension I used to feel is that today's tension comes from my dreams pulling me forward—I've finally learned that's a good thing."

The Tension Catalyst

At its core, every tension point is a good tension. While some are manifested through negative circumstances like damaged relationships or dead-end jobs, when harmonized, they all pull us in the right direction toward a richer, more fulfilling career and life. The tension point between our need to make progress and our need to realize our potential is no exception.

If the pursuit of both is not harmonized, you can end up in a lofty position you have no purposeful attachment to. Sure you can learn the ropes as you climb and qualify yourself for higher and higher positions, but if the skills you gain are out of sync with your natural strengths, you'll end up successful and unenthusiastic—making good money but giving more and more of your life to something out of your zone. You may argue that if the money is good enough, that sort of arrangement is okay. But every year, the statistics tell a different story. When money is the main object of a job, worker dissatisfaction is always above 50 percent—typically, it's pushing 75 percent.

The flip side is that if you don't sync your best skills to an economic engine that produces your necessary income, you end up like an artist I know. He creates beautiful art on aluminum backdrops but hasn't sold a piece in three or four years because he never took the time to figure out how to sync his skill to career progress. He's forced himself to either live on nothing or take any job that pays for his basic needs. It doesn't have to be this way.

By taking these steps to harmonize your career progress with efforts to reach your potential, you'll be moving ever closer to your dream job. And you never know when one more step will take you to that perfect opportunity you've been dreaming of.

Being Noticed vs. Being Esteemed

All sophistication aside, the answer is usually found in your garage.

—Tom Wilder

A t first we all want to be noticed. In time we want to be esteemed, to be respected for our work and who we are as a person. But esteem tends to come at a price many of us are not willing to pay. We're left with accolades but no advocates—recognition but no respect.

Quiet acts of sacrifice and honor—things that happen when nobody's looking—are more likely to bring us respect than a popular decision or action. Esteem or respect doesn't necessarily reward us with a bonus, raise, recognition, or promotion. And therein lies the tension: respect means nothing if others don't recognize our accomplishments.

Let's say you made a conscious decision to allow someone else to gain from an opportunity that could have been yours. This prompted an outpouring of respect from people close to you, but, in the end, someone else got the credit for your accomplishment. A tight little core of insiders knew what you did and respected you for it, but overall it didn't seem to do you much good.

Or let's say you could have made an ambitious move to showcase your skill-set while stepping on toes in the process. Although that would have given you the recognition you missed out on, it might also give your colleagues an unfavorable perception of you. The result: a hollow victory that brought you the credit you craved at the cost of your reputation.

Human nature being what it is, the desire for recognition often trumps the need for respect. While no one likes a cutthroat, no one wants to be a doormat either. The bent toward self-recognition is fostered by a popular culture that preaches the "me gospel." Do what it takes to get the

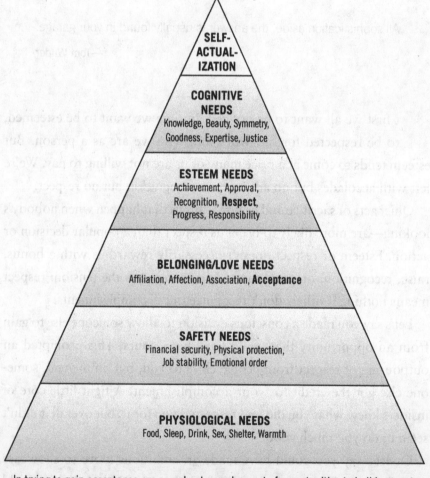

SELF-
ACTUAL-
IZATION

COGNITIVE
NEEDS
Knowledge, Beauty, Symmetry,
Goodness, Expertise, Justice

ESTEEM NEEDS
Achievement, Approval,
Recognition, **Respect**,
Progress, Responsibility

BELONGING/LOVE NEEDS
Affiliation, Affection, Association, **Acceptance**

SAFETY NEEDS
Financial security, Physical protection,
Job stability, Emotional order

PHYSIOLOGICAL NEEDS
Food, Sleep, Drink, Sex, Shelter, Warmth

In trying to gain acceptance, we can cheat ourselves out of opportunities to build respect.
The reverse is also true.

job done—get yours, get recognized. This mentality is driven by more than just the need for praise from your boss or family or friends. Cultural pressures to have more, get more, and be more prey upon a seemingly innocent, natural need to be noticed. Yet, in the end, recognition without respect is an empty disappointment.

The need to be noticed, in and of itself, is not bad. The perversion arises when we over elevate the need by feeding it with the material things of today's culture—when we place greater value on the benefits of recognition than on the benefits of respect.

The tension comes from this: to be successful, you have to make a name for yourself with coworkers, colleagues, and customers; to be respected and esteemed, you have to do it without stepping on toes and elbowing everybody else out of the way. In this chapter you will learn how it's possible to do exactly that.

Respect

By definition, respect is a feeling of deep admiration for someone arising from his abilities, qualities, or achievements. We all have people in our lives we respect deeply. It may be one or both of your parents or grandparents, a coach or teacher, a superior, or even a friend. We see them in light of their achievements, but our feelings for them go much deeper. *How* they achieved what they did is as important as the achievement itself.

Major League outfielder Barry Bonds holds the most coveted record in all of baseball—the most home runs (73) ever hit in a single season. In recent years, however, his achievement has been overshadowed by allegations that he used performance-enhancing drugs to hit all those homers.

There is no doubt that Barry Bonds was an outstanding and greatly respected player, but when this one great achievement is isolated and his professional life scrutinized, many people have questioned the authenticity of his record-breaking career. Barry stands alone for career home runs—and the key word here is *alone*. Not only does he hold the record by himself, he has been publicly alienated because of questions that won't go away about how he attained that record. He has recognition, but his methods cost him respect.

Which is more important?

America's recent economic crisis yields an endless string of examples showing how readily people will sacrifice respect for recognition and reward. During the past few years there were ample warning signs that the housing market bubble was going to pop. Government officials warned that Fannie Mae and Freddie Mac, federal entities that hold the majority of American home mortgages, needed to be reined in. As the value of houses skyrocketed, lenders greedy for more business made risky loans to people who could afford them only if the real estate market kept charging ahead. But no one heeded the warnings. The housing marked imploded, and within the span of two weeks during the summer of 2008, our federal government took over insurance juggernaut AIG, proposed and passed a financial bailout for Fannie and Freddie, and later started distributing billions of taxpayer dollars to ailing car makers.

There was plenty of finger-pointing to go around. The presidential race fueled the fire, with each party accusing the other of not doing more to prevent the economic collapse. But the real culprits turned out to be the CEOs of these massive companies. In the wake of AIG being rescued by the U.S. government's taking a majority ownership share, AIG upper management officials spent more than $440,000 during eight days at an elite California spa. Other CEOs were given the proverbial golden parachutes—some amounting to hundreds of millions of dollars—as they exited their failed institutions, leaving investors penniless after the company stock plummeted.

Why did this happen? We can theorize about the ins and outs of investment banking, buying up bad mortgages, and so forth. But I'm convinced that this economic meltdown occurred because too many business executives went after status, recognition, and power in the eyes of their peers and the public instead of the respect of their investors. They lost sight of their responsibility to manage the wealth of millions of trusting clients and let their egos take over. This is a prime example of how the reckless, self-absorbed pursuit of recognition without respect can corrupt.

An Unsophisticated Answer

I recently had a fascinating conversation with a highly successful operations director for one of the world's top pharmaceutical companies. With more than fifteen years experience in his field, Tom Wilder has methodically improved his expert skill set, advanced his position, and become indispensable in an industry that enjoys grinding up high-level personnel.

Tom enjoys a high standard of living in the Pacific Northwest, with all the spoils of the "Wild West" at his fingertips—great fishing, river kayaking, mountain biking, and snowboarding. His family benefits from his success, flex schedule, and adventurous spirit. But before you roll jealous eyes at Tom's station in life, you should know that none of it was possible without understanding the harmony between winning the respect of others and the recognition of superiors. His perspective may startle you.

"It's a difficult question," he admitted. "But the fact is that I'm not sure there is a distinction between the two—for me, it's more of a singular focus. I'd like to give you a sophisticated answer, but the honest truth is . . . more of a Sunday school answer than a corporate answer . . . My primary mantra is that I don't perform for a group or organization. I perform for an audience of One."

Right off the bat in our conversation, I sensed that Tom had latched on to some keen insight into surviving the corporate trap that says "performance is king." For most people at Tom's level, recognition is the precursor to respect. Everyone knows that you do what it takes to get seen by the boss. If you perform, then respect will follow. Right? Not exactly.

He continued, "My responsibility as a director, the corporate pressure, and so on, create a situation that can leave a person alone among the wolves. Everyone is basically trying to win a job, save a job, or steal a job. There is always pressure to perform. You are surrounded by people whose mantra is 'Success at any cost.' But in the end those things can't and don't last. It's the popular perception that success is only derived from recognition. But that simply is not true. The one truth I've discovered is that recognition fades."

Tom's perspective was refreshing—one I could relate to. I have seen friends and colleagues climb the ladder of success, achieving great things along the way, only to be undercut by an intangible: layoffs, corruption, or a person who is better and will work for less. Pursuing recognition is extremely egocentric. Without a constant diffuser, you can get so wrapped up in yourself that all you see is what you have done—not who you have become. Tom made a great point. But then he threw a curveball.

"In my estimation, personal recognition is a selfish end . . . and when we are in a place where what we do feeds only the self, then we are in a precarious place. Very little can come of our pursuits . . . I've found this to be true time and time again."

"But Tom," I said, "most people don't know anything else. They equate success with recognition. In order to change that perception you have to change their definition of success. How do you explain the idea that success is rooted in achieving respect over recognition?"

He thought for a moment and then replied, "You're right. At some point in this discussion words become useless. I can stand here all day and tell you that seeking recognition is a fruitless endeavor yet convince no one to seek a different path. I can only tell you what I do in my position day after day. I do my best to model respect and honor, and let the chips fall where they may."

His comments started me thinking about the group of snorkelers I watched that morning in the bay. It took me seeing a group of people doing something out of the ordinary to begin to rethink my work/life values. Then it hit me. Tom was a snorkeler!

He operated his work/life according to an adjusted set of corporate perceptions. He had spent time thinking through the ramifications of seeking recognition as an end goal. He had come up with a new set of rules, something that freed him from the pressure of performing for recognition. Like the snorkelers in the bay, Tom was operating by a set of rules that only comes when we think outside the confines of our current circumstances.

Tom wrapped up his discourse with a line that I have contemplated for some time: "The handcuffs of self-esteem can bind us to something we ultimately don't want to be in."

Unlocking the Handcuffs

Tom was describing the pop culture trap that recognition is king. As a successful director, his position elevates him above many of his coworkers in stature and income. This could easily be an impetus to leverage his position to pursue only those benefits that would improve his résumé and lifestyle. But Tom resists this approach.

He views the trappings of culture as handcuffs. While material possessions are not inherently bad, the sole pursuit of them can actually diminish the value of accomplishments. Having a nice boat or a few four-wheelers or a cabin getaway is all fun. There's nothing wrong with collecting them. The danger comes when they are the ends of your means. Your things do not make you more respectable. They are merely fringe benefits of success. The lasting benefits—the benefits that will take your company or career where you'd like it to go—are those tied to others' respect for you. Tom leans hard on this truth.

He has cultivated this approach throughout his career. In his twenties he carried some debt because he wanted to have some of the creature comforts life offered. But now as a husband and the father of three boys, the things that make life exciting are centered more on his family and less on himself. If he did not approach his professional life in this way, his personal life would suffer. You cannot—or, at least, should not—pursue things to satisfy the lusts of self when people depend on you for sustenance, support, and love.

Unlocking the handcuffs translates into understanding your position in life and not allowing the trappings of this world to consume you. What do I mean by position? It could be a few things, actually. Understand that if you are in a position of power and leadership, then you have a responsibility for those you lead. You are a modeler. What will you model? Will you model a life that is consumed with status, gathering all the material things a person in your position is supposed to have? Or will you look for ways to model discernment and moderation, excitement for life and steadfastness?

Then there is the life position to consider. A married person will have a different set of goals from those who are single and can devote all their time to their task. As a young professional you may be able to enjoy some things for a while. But the sooner you realize that material things pass and that people should be the object of your affections, the better. The bottom line here is to remember that whether you are a single executive or a married one, you owe it to yourself and others to rise above the clamoring noise of the culture screaming for your attention. Recognition is not born out of this mentality. True recognition overflows from a life that has its priorities straight.

For Tom, personal goals are great, but they become empty when they advance only him. His goals and decisions are based on family and faith—the things that mean the most in his life.

Tom said, "I know of three people right now—friends of mine—who have either been fired or their marriage is falling apart. The incessant pursuit of self-gratifying things has led them down a path that dead-ends. What good is having everything that recognition and success can afford when you lose those who are closest to you?"

The key principle here is at the core of all we do when we are driven by something. What is it that drives you? Do you desire the esteem of others as the natural consequence of professional recognition? Are you held captive by the handcuffs of esteem?

The Right Decision

It's no easy task to leave pride out of the professional equation. If you do not stand for yourself, no one else will. And every leader must have a certain sense of confidence in his or her approach. But what does this confidence entail? In the end, what should it accomplish? Consider this story from the 1988 Korean Olympics:

Finn class sailor Lawrence Lemieux was poised to do well in the Seoul games—some were even picking him to win the gold in the race for single-handed craft. But in a preliminary qualifying round, Lemieux was faced with a tough decision.

According to a *New York Times* article, the Canadian native was vying for position among the top ten racers to remain in contention for the gold medal. But his chase for first was disrupted when he heard shouting from a Singapore sailor competing in a different class who had drifted off course and capsized in bad weather.

"He was obviously desperate," Lemieux said in an interview. "He had hurt his back and was shouting."[1]

Lemieux did not hesitate. He turned his boat around and aided the injured sailor—relinquishing his pursuit and essentially conceding the race altogether. Joseph Chan was exhausted, separated from his boat, and in serious trouble, with six-foot waves making his position dire.

Lemieux waited with Chan until the rescue boat arrived and then continued the race, finishing in twenty-first place. Some competitors would not see aiding a fellow participant as part of their responsibility. After all, recognition for the race comes at the medal stand, not in aiding another participant and finishing near the back of the pack. Lemieux did not see it that way.

"It just was one of those decisions," he said. "The very first rule is to help people in distress."[2]

For Lemieux, helping Chan was the right thing to do—the top priority above the gold metal. It was not a decision that was in his best interest as a sailor, and it was not a decision he could have taken lightly.

On the one hand, he raced toward the esteem of being cemented in Olympic history as a medal winner. On the other hand, he remembered the well-being of another before his own aspirations. Gold does not always line selfless decisions before us, but that's what makes them priceless. The respect and admiration Lemieux received for his decision will not easily be forgotten. With Olympic fame and a life on the line, the decision was still clear: aid for another instead of glory for self.

In the end, the president of the International Olympic Committee awarded Lemieux the Pierre de Coubertin Medal for sportsmanship. When no one was watching, the Canadian had made a tough decision totally void of self-promotion or gain. The recognition he did gain was not something he aspired to in helping Chan; it was the by-product of respect. Lemieux's decision did not bring the immediate recognition of the masses, but it showcased his noteworthy character. Today, sailing enthusiasts would be hard-pressed to recall who won the Olympic gold that year, but they quickly remember the man who set aside his race plans and earned the respect of the world.

Wholly Simple

Perhaps the harmony we are seeking in this chapter is better described as wholeness. In our attempt to reconcile the tension between the very human need to be recognized with the desire to be respected by our colleagues, we have stumbled upon a profound truth. Respect is not necessarily something that we set out to achieve. Rather, it's the by-product of a life lived in wholeness—a life of integrity.

All sophistication aside, Tom said, "The answer to this conundrum is usually found in your garage."

The garage is absolutely devoid of anything worthy of recognition—especially if your garage looks like mine. For most, the garage is typically the place where toys are collected, where Christmas trees are stored, and where the leftovers of a well-ordered life are hidden away. But for some, the garage is a place where common household duties are carried out and family projects are initiated. For Tom, the garage is his sanctuary.

He is an avid cyclist, a competent bike and car mechanic, and a bit of a rogue craftsman. For him, the garage is a place to execute projects for his wife and boys—it's his laboratory. Most notably, the garage is a secluded place. It is a place where tools and talk radio become his closest and only friends. A place where performance is for an audience of none.

When Tom said the answer to this tension between recognition and respect can be found in your garage, what he meant was that the way you perform in your garage (or basement) when no one is watching reveals the true you. In today's world, compartmentalization—the idea of being one way in your work life and another way in your personal life—is rampant and widely acceptable. Tom, however, makes no such distinction. You are who you are, all the time. We were not created to be walking dichotomies; we are whole beings. This concept sculpts Tom's life.

He believes that the garage—his metaphor for a person's unseen actions—will shape who you ultimately become in the workplace. The "garage you" will ultimately be revealed in the "workplace you." The distinction is this: the passion that drives you to be excellent and true when no one is watching is the same passion that will drive you in your professional life. It is the "whole-of-you" being expressed within both areas of life.

The garage provides the opportunity to put respect first, the opportunity to do something well, not because you are driven by a need to be seen, but because you desire to be good at your core.

Tom described it this way: "You build a shoe rack in your basement to the best of your ability. Your kids see it, your wife loves it, and all of a sudden you see your work life transform." He continued, "Sure, you could skimp on the project and slap something together—it's only a shoe rack for crying out loud. Right? Wrong. It is an extension of you at the most insignificant level, which is also you at a higher level. Your choice to pursue excellence in your basement lays the foundation for you to send that e-mail out that you could have fudged on but decided not to.

"You begin experiencing humanity at a new level. You perform not because you are driven but because you have an inner personal need to do something right and do it well, regardless of what it ends up being for you—regardless of a positive or negative outcome. It is about wholeness—being who you are totally—being who you were meant to be."

And that leads us to Tom's Garage Principles.

Garage Principle #1: "Mind Time" Recognition

Listening to Your Inner Dialogue Reveals the True You.

Tom offered a couple of application handles that help him keep focused on the right things. The first handle he described as "mind time." This is a barometer that tells you how well you are managing your thoughts. Think about it: you spend most of your day in an inner dialog that determines decisions, shapes your world-view, and cultivates your attitude.

"Mind time," said Tom, "answers questions like: Do I spend time lusting after the next best thing—new car, big house, big promotion? Or, am I centered on the things that matter—family, relationship with my wife, and doing good for others?"

The harmony comes from realizing that people will give you recognition if you perform with excellence. The main thing, however, is that you are not driven by the recognition but by the excellent things in life: being whole, serving others, and producing excellence. Instead of living your life in compartments—your work life here, your home life here, your "guy time" persona here—you should seek to be the same person no matter where you are. Being a whole person simply means not being divided—it means being authentic all the time.

Garage Principle #2: Mustard Seed Acknowledgement

Acknowledging Good Things Focuses Our Attention on the Good of Others.

I love Tom's second application handle, the "mustard seed acknowledgement" principle. It dovetails with the "mind time" principle, taking it one step further by giving it action. In order to cultivate an inner life that's focused on the good of others, we must take the time to acknowledge good things. This creates a mindset that is not focused on the self but on others and their betterment.

It's as simple as noticing a selfless act by a coworker or praising your spouse for a job well done. This positive reinforcement is a viable tool used by coaches to establish a culture of optimism on a team. By affirming the good things an individual player does, a coach lifts his status among team members. This in turn elevates the entire team's perspective of that individual player. If that player is already a leader or captain, it galvanizes the team behind leadership they can trust—leadership they will follow no matter what the game dishes out.

Similarly, when the coach heaps praise on the entire team, calling them out for something noteworthy, it engenders an attitude of togetherness. The team sees that when they work together, serving each other in their individual roles, the entire team benefits.

The same is true in professional life. Recognition is not the goal. The goal is raising the level of personal buy-in and corporate productivity by acknowledging people and teams for their positive work. The caveat here is that this cannot be something you simply have on your "Get Respect and Recognition" checklist. It is an ethos—a way of being that establishes a culture for those around you—shaped by a disciplined desire to celebrate the good in all aspects of life, whether it's at home, in the garage, around the dinner table, or around the conference table.

The secret to this principle is seeking the good of others, using your mind time to perpetuate an "others first" inner culture. By seeking the higher good for others, by acknowledging things that are good and true in the lives and events of others, you create inner wholeness that's expressed outwardly in everything you do.

So how can you do this right now? Here are a few tips to get your wheels turning in the right direction.

Five Ways to Be a Mustard Seed Encourager

1. This week at work look for three new ways you can praise those on your team for the job they did.
2. Go out of your way to write a note of encouragement to your spouse at least once this week.
3. Use your lunch break for something other than eating: help a coworker with a project or take a walk outside to clear your head—you'll be surprised to see how a change of scenery for you can have a positive impact on others.
4. When critiquing someone—whether at work or at home—be the person who builds them up, not tears them down.
5. Think before you react. When listening to proposals, reviews, or inquiries, hear out the listener. Anyone can respond quickly to a situation. A good listener goes a long way to create a culture of trust in your personal and private life.

Unearthing a Startling Truth

In this chapter we've attempted to solve the tension between our innate need to be recognized and the deep desire to be respected by others. But Tom's insights revealed that at its core, this tension springs from the false assumption that recognition is something we must have. We've unearthed compelling concepts that have nothing to do with harmonizing our need for personal recognition and our desire to be respected. The irony is that, contrary to what most people believe, respect is not the end game or goal. It is the by-product of a life lived fully—a life lived with integrity. It comes from being wholly you.

In my discussion with Tom, he was almost apprehensive about sharing his findings. But what makes his story and advice so compelling is that it doesn't stem from any kind of personal piety; it comes from a heart that has seen both sides of success and has opted for the one he has found to be more true. Do men and women strive for recognition every day and receive it? Of course. Do men and women fight for respect in their jobs and marriages? Absolutely. But to what end?

Tom realized that attempting to join the two dichotomies ended in frustration. In trying to pursue harmony, Tom inadvertently found himself gaining the respect of coworkers. As he served others in his leadership role, he discovered that leadership is not about lording a position—it is about empowering a team of people to perform well. By lifting others up, he established himself as someone who knows how to get results because people follow him.

A team divided is already defeated. It's the same with the individual. It is impossible to chase after recognition without denigrating your reputation—unless you are especially gifted at masking brazen self-fulfillment. Do not misunderstand me in all of this. I am not saying that recognition is bad. Nor am I saying it is unnatural to want it. I am saying that it should not dictate how you pursue your career, because it will affect how you treat others in the long run.

The two concepts seem as if they contradict each other, but they do not. By pursuing individual harmony we achieve a personal standard by which others measure us. By celebrating the good in others and in everyday circumstances, we cultivate a culture of unity. By monitoring our thoughts and distilling vacant passions, we remain focused on our families and personal relationships—culture's grip is loosened. And once we're free of culture's grip, we are able to realize that recognition all by itself can become deceptive. It can pit us against one another, hobbling our respect for each other.

Having the respect of others is not about divisiveness; it is about unity. It is about seeing the whole picture of a person and placing trust in him or her. For trust is the precursor to respect. It is the foundation of everything good and true—it is what makes us whole.

A Final Thought

Up until this point we have used Maslow's Pyramid as a tool to see what the driving factors in our lives are and how that affects our decisions. According to Maslow, we begin in life being driven by base needs, then we move into more abstract needs such as self-esteem and community, where we are affirmed in our giftedness.

We are going to begin to see something in the next chapter, however, that will literally flip Maslow's ideas upside down. We will discover that our greatest needs may seem personal—driving us toward self-realization. But the reality is that true self-realization is defined as being useful and meeting the needs of others.

As we begin to unravel this idea, we will be confronted with the irony that our greatest need as individuals—as humans—is not a personal need but a corporate one. When we begin to ascend the inverted pyramid, moving *from* a central place of self-realization, we start understanding that self-realization is the starting point in helping meet the needs of others.

Growing Professionally vs. Growing Personally

> I wanted to get paid for being me. But I still hadn't defined what
> that was.
>
> —Summer Scott

Career success comes from pouring everything you have into your job. Personal fulfillment comes from time spent enriching and nurturing your life. Rare is the man or woman who has both, because 80 percent of us spend our days pursuing only one or the other. Why is that? Does pursuit of a successful career demand a high measure of personal sacrifice? Does the quest for personal significance require a high measure of career sacrifice? The answer to some extent is yes on both counts. But the rarity of those who consistently pursue—and ultimately possess—both work success and life significance has less to do with sacrifice than with strategy.

Most people put their professional lives in one category and their personal lives in another. They never go after the two simultaneously, only one at a time. They can't concentrate on professional growth without stunting personal life. And when they focus on personal growth, their career gets left in the dust.

But what would happen if you put professional growth and personal growth in the same category? What would that look like? And could it simplify the pursuits of success and significance by combining them in a single focus? These are questions we must look at if we're to remedy the tension point between professional and personal growth.

Not everyone is naturally growth minded, but at some point we're all forced to grow. You get married and realize the habits of single-hood don't work in a marriage. You take a new job and realize your past experience hasn't taught you everything you need to fulfill your current responsibilities. In these and many other scenarios, you have to grow merely to survive, let alone thrive. And growing is often costly—in time, money, effort, and whatever other resources are at your disposal.

As you try—or feel pressured—to grow professionally and person-ally at the same time, a point of tension soon begins to well up inside. We all experience it eventually—a new relationship coupled with greater work responsibilities; a new baby coupled with a new job; family illness coupled with the prospect of a big new account. When such coupled events take place, the key to harmony is developing traits and skills that are equally valuable in both worlds, your professional and your personal life. You've heard of cross-training in the work-place. This is proficiency cross-training on and off the job. It's the best way to grow as a worker while simultaneously growing as a person. In the end, it's the best way to continually meet new challenges on the job and in life without losing ground in either.

Stepping Back and Setting the Foundation

The foundation for all harmonized growth, according to a Floridian named Summer Scott, begins with knowing yourself. At twenty-nine she found herself on the wrong end of a phone call letting her know an online magazine she was hired to run was closing shop. The news forced a decision she hadn't expected to make. "[The magazine] was something I had planned on doing for the next five to ten years," she confessed. "Then all of a sudden I had to come up with a new plan."

She immediately started surfing the Web, hitting up old contacts, and updating her résumé. "But then I took a step back," Summer explained, "and realized I had a unique opportunity to really take stock of my situation . . . Ever since I was young, I wanted a career that really mattered to me and made a difference in people's lives. I was never really one to just get a job, and I didn't want to do that in my situation, even though I knew I needed to make some money."

During the next two weeks Summer dug deep. "I realized I hadn't really given much thought to who I had become as a person since college. I asked myself, *What happened to what I thought I was going to be doing by now?*"

After graduating from Florida State with a marketing and public relations degree, she'd joined forces with a few friends and launched a business. "I loved the flexibility and we made good money, but I ended up getting out because I didn't want to lose my twenties. It was all-consuming but didn't really matter to me. The success was a nonfactor in the grand scheme of things . . . . Although I was growing professionally, I knew I wasn't moving forward on a personal level."

Summer's next job was testimony to her early professional growth. A top-selling magazine hired her to manage the marketing department for its online counterpart. It was a big job for someone in her mid-twenties. She bloomed in the position and was poised to write her own ticket within the organization. Then the smaller start-up magazine came calling.

"I loved what the new magazine represented. It was about something that mattered to me more so than where I was." She jumped ship for the new opportunity. "It was about more than the new opportunity being a better fit with my personal desires; it was a much more flexible and entrepreneurial job. I could work from home and was basically handed the keys to the building. [The founders] told me to take the magazine where I thought it should go."

Summer once again put everything she had into her job, now with a renewed sense of passion. She felt like one of the owners of the project. Her professional skills and personal passions were in alignment with the founders'—it was the perfect fit. Or so it seemed.

The next thing she knew she'd gotten a phone call pulling the plug, the words like lead weights thudding in Summer's brain and echoing in her heart. "After I got the call I felt disoriented and confused," she said. "This was supposed to be 'the job' for me. Now the only things left from it all were lingering doubt and hurt."

Summer had a few choices. She could repeat the routine of blasting her résumé out to potential clients and employers or take a more organic approach to her professional growth—one steeped in personal reassessment. Summer chose the latter.

What should have been the ideal job—fulfilling her professionally and personally—was snatched out from under her. But all was not lost. Tough as it was to absorb a professional blow like that, Summer saw it as a chance to reevaluate what made her tick: "In hindsight I see that I had let this new job define me—but it was not my own. Moving forward, I kept asking myself, *What's my plan? Where do I go from here?* I wanted to get paid for being me. But in some ways I still hadn't defined what that was."

The ancient Greek philosophers loved to use the aphorism, "Know thyself." In today's culture this phrase conjures up cliché images of young idealists who strike out on a journey, across the United States or Europe perhaps, in search of their "true self." This somewhat simplistic approach to self-realization is not totally off base. Exotic journeys let you discover how you respond under duress. It helps you gauge your overall temperament and gain insight into your personal worldview.

In similar fashion, the life journey we're all on demands much from us daily. Our personal experiences fashion and force us into self-discovery that isn't always pleasant. But the hurt it may bring is not an end; it's a beginning. It's the opportunity to step back and regain our footing, an opportunity to find our bearing and plot a new course. It's the opportunity to allow the confluence of our personal and professional worlds to surge together—making two worlds flow in harmony.

Integrating Hurt into Your Career

Our compartmentalized lives have one area for work and another for our personal lives. We get into the routine of grinding it out at work while unplugging from the rest of the world, sequestering our passions and skills. This makes it difficult to get a clear vision of yourself as a total person. It often takes a major setback in order to gain that clarity and perspective and reevaluate your career path. Thus the potentially immense value of a career disappointment is the impetus for change.

The great writer C. S. Lewis referred to pain as God's "megaphone to rouse a deaf world." Think of it as a chance to take a break from the routine and assess the situation with fresh understanding.

Summer found herself in a place of hurt. She had wrapped herself up in a project that was not hers. Though she engaged her job *with* passion, it was not *her* passion. The disappointing result gave her the chance to take a step backward, regain her focus, and ask herself some important questions:

- What am I most passionate about?
- What are my core talents?
- Does this job engage those talents to the fullest?

- What do I enjoy the most in life?
- How do I want to be remembered?

Up to this point Summer had relied on professional training to pave her career path. Her experience and education taught her to take the initiative in finding work. Her willingness to assume risk enabled her to take certain steps others wouldn't be brave enough to try—to quit a high-paying venture to satisfy her longing for personal and professional growth.

But personal pain has a way of botching up our neat plans. It is only a matter of time before life takes a turn and we find ourselves in the middle of a divorce or a layoff or dealing with the loss of a family member. It was a combination of events for Summer. The situation might have been different if she'd lost this job a few years earlier when life was hitting on all cylinders. In reality her professional and personal lives were mirroring each other. She was hobbled by the lack of fulfillment from both sides.

"My parents' breakup and imminent divorce had me reeling," she admitted. "Most days I felt purposeless, but I knew that I had to keep going. The situation with them was part of the reason I decided to take a break from career pursuits and tend bar."

Through her pain Summer has taken the high road regarding her current work/life situation. Instead of throwing her hat back into the career ring right away, Summer took a year off to tend bar at an upscale restaurant near her home. A step backward? Perhaps. A bit embarrassing for someone of Summer's caliber? Probably. But the important thing is that instead of continuing down a career path that only satisfied one layer of needs—professional—Summer set out to lay a foundation based on the values and ideals that made her who she was. Pain was the catalyst for Summer's reevaluation period. But do we have to wait for pain to motivate us? What preventative measures can we take before career fallout?

Fallout Prevention

Most people aren't as lucky as Summer. They don't have the luxury of tending bar for a year to reevaluate their passions and goals. A mortgage and a family don't allow much wiggle room. But if you are reading this and saying, "I'm just starting out in life and want to be sure I am on the right track," or perhaps you are in that hard place that exists between careers, or you realize you're headed down the wrong career path and want out—what then? There are steps you can take to prevent a cycle of decisions that land you in the middle of a career path that's out of harmony with your personal goals and aspirations.

Summer told me the story of her friend, Jen, a highly paid accountant in New York City. "She has a cute apartment and is in the center of a great culture, with tons to do," explained Summer. "But she hates who she's become."

Jen now sees herself in an impossible position. She's worked hard to develop skills that have empowered her to achieve a high level of success. But she ransomed her soul to get it.

Her tension is more pronounced than Summer's. She is enjoying the success of working hard, but she's empty inside. We all know a "Jen." It may be us. But what is the logical conclusion of Jen's setup? We're quick to justify overworking in a job that we care little about because it satisfies our quest for status or wealth or a bit of fame. Yet all the while we waste away on the inside.

In his essay "De Profundis," Oscar Wilde admitted this at the end of his life:

I forgot that every little action of the common day makes or unmakes character, and that therefore what one has done in the secret chamber one has some day to cry aloud on the housetop. I ceased to be lord over myself. I was no longer the captain of my soul, and did not know it.

We don't simply make decisions to work longer; we make decisions to eliminate certain joys of life. We don't simply decide to chase after a promotion we don't really want; we make decisions to drift further and further from who we really are. As Oscar Wilde famously lost himself in hedonistic pleasure, we lose ourselves in careers that strip us of our personal passions and dignity.

Preventing career fallout is as easy as asking yourself the questions Summer is asking herself during her sabbatical. Write these questions on a card and post it next to your computer or by your bed. Allow these questions to become your personal rubric for deciding which career path to pursue.

- Am I passionate about this job?
- What personal value am I pursuing by accepting this position?
- Will this career enhance or detract from my legacy?
- Do I get excited to go to work?
- Does this career bring self-fulfillment (joy)?

Even if you are a career veteran, these questions can help you find clarity, reaffirm your current position, or incite you to make a change you've been putting off for far too long. You don't have to take a year off and tend bar to change career directions, but it does make for a great story.

I Hate Math

A few pages back we met Summer's friend, Jen, the New York accountant. Jen is the type of person who pursues a job for reasons unrelated to her true passions. As a highly paid professional Jen is equipped with all the knowledge she needs to achieve success—but at the cost of her joy and happiness.

Summer represents the type of person who sees her career veering from the path she intended to follow. She and Jen have grown into skill sets that represent their natural professional interests and abilities. In developing her specific skill set, however, Jen has sequestered her professional skills from her personal passions.

On the one hand, Jen is successful. On the other, she loathes who she's become. There is no harmony between her personal and professional life. If she continues down this path—as her professional success stifles personal growth—she will lose herself totally.

Jen is not alone. Every day countless people enter career fields because they are gifted or receive high marks in a certain area. But this approach is dangerous. When you make career decisions just because you're good at something, you can limit yourself. Let me explain.

I hate math. I earned decent grades, but I was far from the budding physicist who couldn't wait to tackle new formulas and problems. Consequently, I avoided a career where math was a core value. Instead, I looked for a career path that would satisfy both my love for working with people and my desire to grow a business.

My goals extend beyond the idea of just holding down a job. I seek total fulfillment in what I do professionally and personally. Because I'm passionate in both areas, my work is not like work—it's almost a guilty pleasure.

When we set out to get educated for the sake of a job, our career/life tension grows. Granted, the end result may be an MBA or excellent certifications. But what is the point if all that leaves us feeling as Jen did? The goal should be to pursue growth in both areas of life.

There is actually an upside to Jen's predicament. Like so many people who find success without happiness, Jen has the opportunity to turn her situation into a positive. The unhappiness and loneliness that first appeared in the professional realm have now spilled over into her personal life. Sad as the situation is, it's teaching Jen a valuable lesson that she can flip to her advantage.

Jen is faced with a decision that straddles the professional/personal divide. She now understands that she can't compartmentalize the two worlds and has a great opportunity to do something about it. This is where growth happens: when we are faced with a seemingly impossible situation and make the tough decision to better ourselves personally.

This is exactly where Summer is in her life. Her professional and personal lives have aligned, forcing her to reevaluate both paths. In some ways Jen's circumstance is much harder. She recognizes the shortcomings of her current path but isn't forced to make a life-altering decision.

No matter where we find ourselves in life, the decision for change is up to us—though it often doesn't feel that way. We find this to be true in Summer's situation. Her catalyst moment came when she made a decision to grow. Summer could have just sent out résumés and continued to leverage her career growth in order to find another well-paying job. But she chose to step back. Now she's enjoying a respite from the grind of career mongering and is able to see with equal clarity both the personal and professional consequences of her decisions.

Jen's catalyst moment may never happen. If not, it's safe to assume that she has chosen the path of least resistance, which often causes the most life tension. But what would happen if Jen chose to seize this catalyst moment? What if she walked away from her empty pursuits to follow the path that allowed her to blossom personally and professionally?

These are the growth moments we all face at some point. We must choose to grow or to stagnate. Our professional circumstances are personal barometers. We grow in both by seizing the opportunities that present themselves—making the tough decisions that reveal our true selves.

Here are two key goals leading to personal and professional growth.

Goal #1: Get Paid for Being Who You Are

It may be possible to get a job that affords you nice things in life. But as we've seen with Jen, that kind of life can leave you empty and alone. Summer's goal was to eventually get paid for being herself. This will sound impossible to some of you. "What do I have to offer that would warrant a paycheck?" But think on this: every one of us is designed with specific gifts and passions. Our culture does its best to tell you to be this or that, leaving many people disillusioned when they find they can't achieve the kind of success popular culture says we all deserve by playing the part culture demands of them.

Summer said she always wanted to help people—even from the time she was a young teenager. That desire never left her; it just matured. The real magic in life happens when you can identify what gives you goose bumps, what gets you excited to be a part of it, or what makes you tear up when no one is watching.

Harnessing your core passions and turning them into a career path isn't just something for the young creative types. It's what everyone should aspire to from the outset. But most of us, like Jen, have bought the lie of culture that predetermines our success and personal satisfaction by default.

How do you discover your core passions and skills? It's a question that demands some exploratory action on your part. Here's an action list that will help you determine your core passions and skills:

- *Dig into your past.* Talk to your parents and siblings about the things you used to care about when you were younger. This is valuable insight for determining your natural proclivities. Were you a natural leader? Did you always have a way with words?
- *Dig into your passions.* What moves you now? What subjects are you naturally drawn to? Who inspires you most? What subjects do you find yourself

exploring in your spare time? Of the things that get you most excited, which ones carry over from personal to professional life?

- *Dig into your developed skills.* Like Summer and Jen, you have gained experience throughout your career that will help you determine what you are and are not good at. List the skills that come naturally to you and that serve as personal assets. Then list the skills that have proved to be useless or that you're not good at. These will help you determine the path you should avoid, thus narrowing the field of possibilities.
- *Dig into your compliment box.* In what areas do you receive the most compliments from people? Does your boss seek you out for information or advice in a certain area? What do you feel you know more about than most people? Have you ever received encouragement from a coach, professor, or teacher that you filed away?

Goal #2: Learn to Influence Yourself

By learning to influence yourself you will be able to engage your career and relationships at a deeper level. This is a difficult goal. Not all of us are good self-evaluators. We're so busy pushing through our careers that we only pause for performance reviews twice a year. Yet this element of growth is crucial to achieve self-realization.

Cutting Through the Noise

Each day we are influenced by our superiors, our friends, television ads—you name it, and if you come in contact with it, it's probably influencing your life. Cutting through outside influences begins by separating yourself from them. Without getting overly mystical about this, you must seek out times of silence and solitude.

The complete absence of sound is a natural simplifier. It eliminates the distractions of television, radio, cell phone, computers, and even family. Left solely to your own quiet thoughts, you'll find your life lies exposed before you. Without the intrusions of the outside world, you are able to think deeply about your life, your goals, and the decisions you must make.

Solitude generally accompanies silence but does not demand it. Solitude, especially in the context of our discussion here, can be a number of things. It can be a secluded place you go to think. It can be a country drive, a quiet hike, or an hour of snorkeling. In a more general sense, it can even be six months tending bar. Solitude can be a superb life equalizer, settling the wire so you can take the next step.

Summer's hiatus is her solitude—her time of silence, her way of cutting through the noise of life and getting her bearing. It is her secluded place that allows her to gain new perspective on past decisions and to lay out plans for a new direction. It is her chance to see that the lessons learned from losing her job with the online magazine are lessons that will help her grow personally—harmonizing the tension that existed in both aspects of her life. Summer is able to influence others as a result of her new direction, which in turn provides a healthy confidence boost for her career.

Flipping the Pyramid

The perfect place to be is this place of self-realization Summer is experiencing. Thinking back to Maslow's pyramid, self-realization was at the top of the pyramid.

But as you move forward from the top of the pyramid, things begin to change. You begin working from a place of influence, engaging others within your professional and private life. Instead of striving for elements of self-need, such as personal safety, belonging, and self-esteem, your focus turns outward. Others are now the beneficiaries of

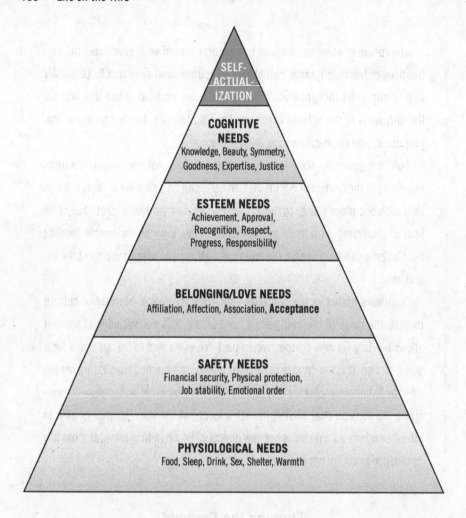

your confidence and self-realization. This position is one of knowing instead of searching, of character strength instead of an attitude that drives you to dominate.

Self-realization enables you to leverage your best assets to engage others. As we found earlier, Summer can influence others at a deeper level because she sees herself clearly now.

Summer now works from a place of self-knowing, has a clearer vision of what she's going after, and is confident in the skills she's collected along the way to achieve her goals. She confidently interacts

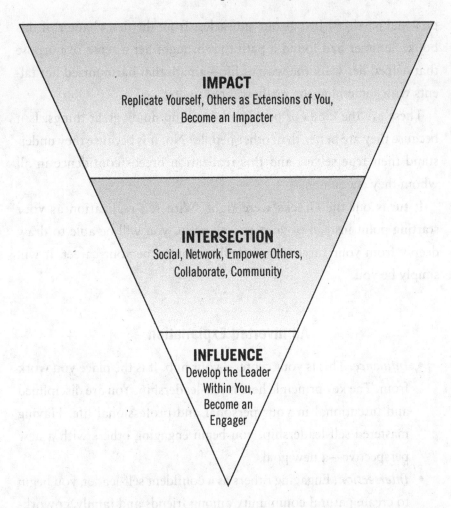

IMPACT
Replicate Yourself, Others as Extensions of You,
Become an Impacter

INTERSECTION
Social, Network, Empower Others,
Collaborate, Community

INFLUENCE
Develop the Leader
Within You,
Become an
Engager

with people of like minds and passions, helping them to achieve their goals and reach their points of self-realization. Rather than being a needy and uncertain liability, Summer is now an asset to others.

Hear that sound? It's the sound of harmony welling from Summer's life. Her self-realization is a benefit to others, an extension of that person. Instead of one person heading off in an ill-fated direction because he or she lacks life vision, you now have a host of people who learn and grow together. People who come across Summer will encounter a young woman who has reconciled her work skills with her personal passions. Just as our snorkelers from the first chapter of this book, Summer had found a path that brought her a sense of purpose that helped her walk the wire of life—a path that harmonized her talents with something she really wanted to do.

These are the kinds of people who end up doing great things. Is it because they are better than other people? No. It is because they understand their true selves, and this realization breeds confidence in all whom they encounter.

It turns out the Greeks were right. With self-realization as your starting point instead of your ending point, you will be able to draw deeply from your career. But it will no longer be your career. It will simply be you.

An Inverted Explanation

- *Influence.* This is your center—your hub. It is the place you work from. The key principle here is self-leadership. You are disciplined and intentional in your personal and professional life. Having mastered self-leadership, you begin engaging others with a new perspective—a new goal.
- *Intersection.* Engaging others as a confident self-leader, you begin to create natural community among friends and family, coworkers and clients. You seek to empower others in their work, seeking their success and ultimately their own self-realization. You are a collaborator; your professional acumen is enhanced because you are confident enough to take as well as give feedback. In short, you are pouring into others; infusing yourself into them. This results in a deep, significant impact.
- *Impact.* Impact is the goal. Your personal and professional engagement begins to bear fruit. You are replicating yourself in others. In work this means that your colleagues or employees become

extensions of you. The need to micromanage disappears. Personally you are the mentor, and your life directly impacts those closest to you as you model the confidence, strength, and grace of someone who understands that the tensions in life are merely opportunities to give life harmony instead of dissonance.

Helping Yourself vs. Helping Others

No one is going to drop significance on my lap. I know that
success and significance are different . . . achieving one helped
me pursue the other.

—Megan Underwood

I t is simple physics, really. A fire cannot materialize without ignition.
Ignition comes from friction between two hard objects. The result is a
spark. From a spark comes the flame. In life, it's the motion of a person
that ignites passion; it is that passion that fuels that person's endeavors.
But what if the spark dies? Whence, then, comes the passion—the ideas
that stir you to action?

Motion. Your mind is in a state of homeostasis, so to speak—constantly regenerating ideas and thoughts. But without being fed, thoughts
and ideas can move from dynamic to static. If you don't use it, you lose
it. You must constantly feed your mind to remain dynamic in your
work and life.

Marketplace success follows the same basic principle. You cannot
stay vibrant in your business role forever without some kind of leaven-
ing—something to feed that need for growth. At some point along the
way—in some fashion—you must be willing to pour into yourself to
achieve success.

You must be intentional about making yourself a better person, whether that means furthering your education, taking an extended international trip, or learning a complementary skill set. Success in life is the by-product of self-discipline; you'll rarely find one without the other. But there's more to making yourself better than spending enormous amounts of time and money enhancing your abilities.

Making yourself a better person also consists of serving your fellow man. Helping others—sacrificing time and energy for them—adds high value to the greater culture and makes you a more significant part of it.

To advance in any endeavor you must invest in yourself and your efforts. To stay ahead in any endeavor you must help others along the way. It's a balancing act whereby you fill up with one hand and pour out with the other. You must continually be filled and be filling in order to achieve both success and significance. This chapter will show you how to do this on a regular basis.

Community Servant

Megan Underwood found a successful way to help others while helping herself. When I spoke with Megan on this topic, she had some perceptive and fascinating insights.

"In today's market, sustainability has taken on a new meaning," she said. "It's not enough for a company to just focus on what matters to the corporate body . . . it must take into account the greater culture. Sustainability isn't a question of being profitable at any cost—it is about helping the community, helping others. In a nutshell, the main requirement for businesses today is social responsibility."

Megan sought a new way to influence society following several years in the Wall Street trenches. After making a name for herself in the corporate banking world, Megan made intentional career moves in order to distill her passion for corporate finance into something that would affect the future. That something was teaching.

Even though Megan had clear opportunities to further her career and pad her checking account, she chose to apply her keen ability to the future of her industry by investing in the next generation. It was a socially responsible move that demanded a new mind-set—a counter-cultural philosophy that lifts up human virtue and social sustainability rather than the pursuit of ego. Megan was giving back instead of taking what she could.

Megan's comments about social responsibility are not empty. She is not leading with mere sound bites; she is leading with her life. And the industry is better for it.

In light of what has happened to our national markets in recent years, the idea of socially responsible companies is a welcome para-digm shift. The recent economic malaise had government officials and economic gurus passing the blame around like a hot potato. No one would take responsibility for the corruption, lack of account-ability, and the disappearance of integrity into the black hole that came to characterize the top ranks of America's banks and govern-ment programs. The tragic results of these actions on the nation's economy—and the global economy—brought about a day of reckon-ing. Suddenly everybody demanded a change from the old mind-set of "me first."

Megan's comments on sustainability were prophetic. The corporate hierarchy had not included the local community, let alone the global one. It was concerned with the bottom line above all else. This type of corporate mind-set was destined to hit bottom eventually. That time has arrived.

A New Bottom Line

There's a new trend surfacing in the corporate world that reflects the underpinnings of my discussion with Megan. Success, as it has been traditionally defined, is morphing into a paradigm of sustainability. Tim

Sanders—author and former chief solutions officer at Yahoo!—talked about the new corporate ethos—the triple bottom line.

The triple bottom line (3BL) concept was introduced in the mid-nineties. It creates a more sustainable business model by focusing on three areas that measure success: economic, environmental, and social. Economics traditionally has been the prime metric for success, but the paradigm has shifted. The idea suggests that *shareholders* in companies have begun to view themselves as *stakeholders*, which takes the focus off of shareholder profit and puts it on stakeholder interest.

The 3BL point of view calls for the corporate world to grow a conscience and make decisions based on more than economic gain. I hope this means a new era in business is upon us—an era defined by helping others and working for the good of the common man, rather than selfish gains at any cost.

But how does the idea of corporate sustainability apply to me personally? Glad you asked. The answer leads us to the concept of significance.

Sustainable Significance

We'll talk more about significance in the final chapter, but it's important for our discussion here as it relates to helping others. First we must debunk the idea that significance is found in economic success. People are not significant because they can bring in the cash. True personal significance is measured in terms of a person's impact on others.

The coach who spends twenty years with a high school football team in middle America is no less significant than the entrepreneur from Silicon Valley. Their bank accounts have nothing to do with living a life that matters. In fact, the entrepreneur may spend his nights popping sleeping pills because he can't find meaning in what he does; all the while the football coach sleeps serenely. Why? Because the entrepreneur is focused purely on himself and what he can take from this life, while the coach is pursuing others and the impact he can make upon the lives he comes in contact with.

The coach considers how he can improve his team. His motivation is based on a team concept rather than on what will benefit him personally. He carries a responsibility that acts as a sort of accountability. He knows his decisions affect a team of fifty or more players—any decision made outside of that framework would be exposed.

By contrast, the business mogul is motivated by a more tangible outcome—money. Citizens of the corporate world commonly disregard others completely, garnering praise for doing whatever it takes to achieve a robust bottom line. This kind of behavior may produce profits, but it's no way to build something genuinely and lastingly significant.

When the coach looks back over his years at the high school, he will be able to name people on whom he has had a direct impact. When he surveys his life, he will find comfort in the fact that the years he spent pouring himself into the football program and those young boys were worth it. He will look throughout the community and see those players as men with their own families, incorporating the same principles that governed his team. That is sustainable significance.

It is important here to consider the roll that community plays in developing personal significance. Psychologist Dr. Henry Stein, director of the Alfred Adler Institute of Northwestern Washington, provided the following insight.

It is helpful to distinguish between positive and negative striving. Positive striving would be in the direction of overcoming difficulties, gradual self-development, and improving a situation for mutual benefit. The individual moves ahead in reality (a "horizontal" movement), and his significance is confirmed by other people. By contrast, negative striving would be wanting power over others, superiority over others, dominating others, and seeking Godlike supremacy. The individual merely moves up and down in his fantasy (a "vertical" movement), and his significance is largely imagined.[1]

To put it plainly, Dr. Stein observes that when people strive for positive things and seek to overcome obstacles for the benefit others, other people confirm their significance.

On the other end of the cultural spectrum, Oprah Winfrey made a similar observation: "The key to realizing a dream is to focus not on success but significance—and then even the small steps and little victories along your path will take on greater meaning." Oprah took the idea of Stein's "strivings" and made them personal.

What are you striving for? Is it a dream? What is that dream? Is it completely self-fulfilling? Are you making room in your dream for other people? Oprah differentiates between success and significance—significance holds the higher value, while success is just a positive result from working hard.

If significance is an "others oriented" ideal that takes root in the community you foster day by day, then it's time to evaluate your environment. Who is it that makes up your community? When it is all said and done, significance that lasts is built with people, for people, and sustained by people. If you do not have your very own peanut gallery to cheer you on, and if the only thing you are pouring into is a pint glass, it's time to start expanding your personal influence base. Don't get caught settling into complacency.

A Base Trap

We have an instinctive need for measured success, which in the business world generally means success measured at the bottom line. This is the base need on Maslow's pyramid. It's interesting to note that many people stop right there at the base need of physical and measurable success. Yet this is only the beginning of our journey. If we want to strive for our fullest potential, we need to be operating out of a place of self-realization.

There's a trap in this pyramid, and it's the trap of success. Measured success satisfies our "safety and belonging" needs. That's why we feel all warm and fuzzy when we finally have the house we've been eyeing for years. Or, now that we can finally commute in an $80,000 6-Series BMW and not the $20,000 Camry, we have arrived. These things are traps. When our needs are being met, it is easy to fall into complacency.

But then we start to feel that nagging sense deep inside that there's got to be something more. If we don't, then the spoils of success have blinded us. I hope you're not trapped in complacency. I hope you suspect there's something more to life than the material trappings of success and that you will look around for ways to leverage what you have accomplished for something that will be lasting.

Look at Maslow's pyramid again. Are you trapped near the base? Are you content merely to meet the creature needs of life and forgo seeking significance?

As you look at this pyramid, notice that material success stretches high up into the Esteem Needs category. This is where you begin to receive the respect from your peers. You identify yourself with your job because you are proud of what you have accomplished, and people start patting you on the back, telling you how great you are and that it's all blue sky and sunshine in Successville.

The problem is that the line of success stretches no further. It fails to extend into self-realization. Why? Personal success is the two-headed monster that says, "Congratulations, you've made it. There's nothing left to do." This is the lie that will derail you in your pursuit of significance.

Leadership guru John C. Maxwell asserts that success in leadership

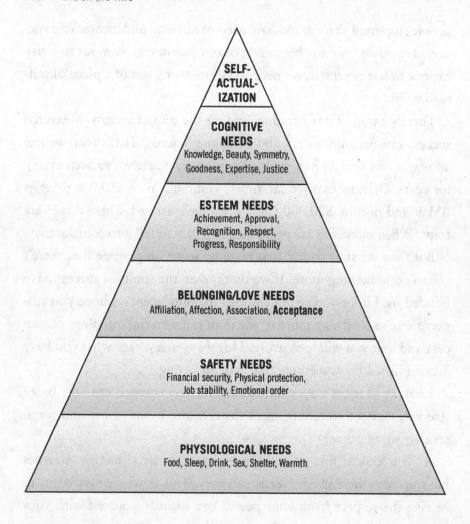

is a by-product of a superb supporting cast. For John, personal success is not a lonely affair. He said, "If you're lonely at the top, then you're not doing something right." Leadership is pointless if there are no followers.

If you are content with your success because you've attained all the status symbols of the "successful," then you are the lonely leader. You are at the top, but no one cares.

Be the Difference

Megan, our banker-turned-teacher, saw no sustainable future in an industry that hails monetary success as its only significance. But not everyone has to quit a job and seek out community work to find significance. It may be as simple as starting a mentor program at the office for aspiring college students. Or teaching a class in prison. Or coaching a sports team.

Megan had achieved a level of success that allowed her to dictate her work schedule, enabling her to rediscover her passion for teaching. When the time was right, she had no problem saying good-bye to Wall Street—she knew that her true worth was found in a career path that poured into others.

I cannot emphasize enough the trap that our society lays out for hard-working people. Sadly, success in our culture is measured by the accumulation of things. The more frightening fact is that people draw their significance from those things.

If that's where you are you've got to change your mind-set. Be intentional about seeking out the work situations that will allow you to pour into others. The tension that results will be the constant pull to accomplish great things for yourself while also finding ways to pour into others for the greater good.

When I asked Megan for insights into her pursuit of significance, she simply said, "I just keep telling myself that I have to *be* the difference. No one is going to drop significance on my lap. I know that success and significance are different . . . achieving one helped me pursue the other."

Megan is at a point where she no longer has to figure out what significance looks like. But many people are still caught up in the culture trap. To them—and maybe you—monetary success feels significant.

But that's a false feeling, the lie of a culture that will sell you a glacier in Greenland if you're willing to buy it. The temporary high from achieving can lead to bad decisions and a muddled view of others and a warped view of success. Consider these common myths:

Myths of Success

- *Success equals wealth.* Don't assume you've dodged the "success traps" of our culture just because you don't drive a new BMW. For many, success can be as simple as being able to support yourself full-time by doing something you love. Though life success, as our culture defines it, may keep you content, that very contentment keeps you from enjoying the far greater life-gifts that significance offers. Contentment, then, is a learned behavior; it pacifies us but does not offer true happiness. Think about Mother Teresa. She had significance. Her happiness was not based on a false contentment. It was based on doing something that matters, no matter what the material value. This is when true significance is gained.

- *Success means you have arrived.* Everyone wants to be successful. Once people find success they don't want to upset their mojo by changing the way they do things. This myth goes back to our earlier point about Maslow's pyramid—once we land somewhere in the middle, we forget about moving on to the top. To truly arrive in life is to find a deep sense of significance. Success means you have achieved. Significance means you have made a difference.

- *Material things define success.* We already know that success does not equal wealth. You can experience genuine success regardless of your tax bracket. But in today's professional world, competition is fierce. The accepted way to prove you're better than the other guy is to achieve greater financial success—get more stuff. Shallow and false as it is, this myth goes even further. It's not just about getting more stuff, it is defining yourself by the stuff you have. We become socially bankrupt when we measure humanity by the amount of material possessions someone has collected.

Reflect on these two important insights.

Key Insight #1:
Sustainable endeavors consider both the bottom line and the lives of others.

Sustainability is the buzzword here. The business world is moving toward a new sustainable paradigm. Big business is not just about the bottom line; it considers people. This new movement of the professional marketplace is coming at a great time. As our markets are rebuilt because of greedy, corrupt leadership, it's encouraging to see a move toward valuing people.

The marketplace is becoming more organic and holistic. It is taking a new stance on corporate responsibility, which trickles down into organizational leadership. Soon this new ethos will begin to redefine success. But in the meantime, you must take the lead.

Whatever you set out to do professionally, seek a career path that takes this new view of success to heart. Simply working in an industry that is cognizant of the environment and people elevates you to a level of significance.

Don't get tricked into thinking you have to quit your job right now or look for a new career path. If you are pursuing a successful career, that's great. Keep going. Just begin to adopt the idea that wherever you are, you can be a difference-maker. Start by applying your skill set in a way that will benefit more than just your job performance.

Look for new ways to influence people with your skills. If you are a graphic artist, then start a summer camp for at-risk teenagers and ask your employer to

---

get behind it. Pour yourself into others, make your company a more sustainable organization, and achieve the type of success that affects a whole community.

Key Insight #2:
Significance demands self-sacrifice.

When I spoke with Megan, she was almost jubilant about her new circumstances. Teaching is her sweet spot. But getting there demanded sacrifice. Megan has the skill set to make a substantial amount of money, yet she chose to pursue a career that allows her to pour into others every day. It's a trade-off Megan made willingly. But her nonchalance concerning self-sacrifice does not diminish the fact that she gave up something prized by her former peers to get what she knew was far more important.

Think back to our coaching analogy. Similar to a teacher, the football coach spends his time pouring into athletes. He shapes boys into young men but does so at a price to himself. Coaching demands countless hours alone in a film room with other coaches. It demands late nights prepping game plans and long bus rides away from the family. It is a grueling endeavor that demands self-sacrifice.

The point is that anything worth doing that has lasting impact will demand self-sacrifice at some level. Whether you are the mega-successful entrepreneur considering a career change to seek significance, or the nine-to-five banker looking to use your talents for meaningful community impact, you will sacrifice something. It could be your hefty salary; it may be time away from your family to finish that master's degree.

Significance comes at a price. After I spoke with the snorkelers, I realized that in order for them to incorporate something of value into their lives, they had to make some serious personal and professional concessions. But the result was obviously worth it. Professional significance is no different. For many of you reading this, it will come on the heels of success, but it will demand that you push further in a way you are not used to pushing. It will stretch you out of the comfort of the familiar and plunge you into a world that is new and hard and beautiful. No one ever said life on the wire was easy. But the great things in life never are.

An Odd Insight

I am not usually given to highly poetical moments. But all this talk of "significance at a price" reminds me of my writer, who likes somewhat odd poetry. Several times while we were compiling ideas for this book, he would reference some random poet or an old piece of prose that he enjoyed. One in particular comes to mind at this moment.

It is a poem by the great T. S. Eliot, a Harvard graduate, a publishing executive for most of his life, and the winner of the Nobel Prize in Literature. One of his most celebrated works is called *Four Quartets*. Don't worry; I am not going to parse each poem in the set. I simply want to draw your attention to a section of the one called "East Coker."

The poem unravels over five sections and gets a bit too depressing for my taste. But the redeeming part that applies to our discussion is a section that alludes to a World War II hospital.

> Our only health is the disease
> If we obey the dying nurse
> Whose constant care is not to please
> But to remind of our, and Adam's curse
> And that, to be restored, our sickness must grow worse.[2]

I will spare you the final few stanzas, but the point Eliot is making is excellent. It is the idea that anything worthy of doing must come through suffering and tolerance. By suffering I do not mean to imply that you must undergo physical pain. But you will have to sacrifice things you think you may deserve. You will have to continue to pour into people even when it would make more sense to keep building yourself up.

In the end, the tension between finding success and experiencing significance will be offset by a purposeful imbalance of constantly pouring into others as quickly as knowledge and experience are pouring into you. Tim Sanders, author of the best-selling book *Love Is the Killer App,* said:

> Learn as much as you can as quickly as you can and share your knowledge aggressively; expand your network of people who share your values and connect as many of them with each other as possible; and, perhaps most important, be as openly human as you can be and find the courage to express genuine emotion in the harried, pressure-filled world of work.[3]

Finding significance is all about other people. It is not what you can get from them; it is what you can give. Take another look at our inverted pyramid. As you move out from a position of self-knowing you begin to encounter other people—let's call this "social interaction." Interacting with people is your opportunity to empower them by sharing yourself: your pain, your victories—you.

When you begin to interact with other people and establish relationships, you become an impetus for change in their lives. You are giving to them what your life experience has given you, which makes you part of their life experience, which begins the exponential influence of your life. This is not a small matter. Great leaders are the ones who can draw a whole galaxy of lineage lines from their relationships.

This is vividly apparent in sports as assistant coaches are mentored, move on to become head coaches, and, in turn, begin the process all over again with their coaching staffs. In community there is growth; in isolation there is only stagnation.

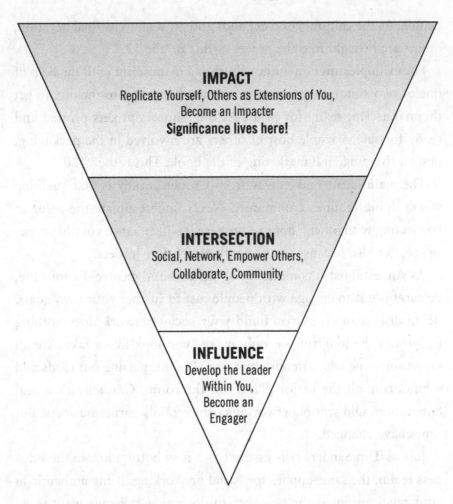

Think about the people you know who are widely successful. The majority of them did not get to where they are without a community around them, mentoring them and providing timely advice.

It Takes More Than One

Culture Makers, by Andy Crouch, is a recent book about people who create culture. Crouch introduced the concept of "the three, the 12 and the 120."[4] The idea is that any kind of successful cultural good—a book or business or movie—begins with the collaboration of three people. As the cultural good expands and grows into its final iteration, others are brought into the process—this is "the 12."

For example, after an author finishes a manuscript with the help of one or two editors, then other people are brought into the mix to get the manuscript ready for print. As the manuscript gets printed and ready for sale, a whole host of others are involved in the packaging, design, shipping, and marketing of the book. This is the "120."

The main idea to take away from Crouch's study is that anything worth doing requires community. Never underestimate the value in connecting with others, not just because it will enhance your life experience, but also because you can influence future leaders.

As you establish a community of mentors and mentees in your life, be careful not to engage with people just to further your own goals. Being disingenuous as you build your social network does nothing for you in the long run—it only makes you look like a fake. We all know someone who attends every social event, passing out cards and schmoozing all the major players in the room. Granted, it's a real temptation. Old school networking can certainly garner business. But times have changed.

Just as Tim Sanders tells us there is a new bottom line in the business realm, the same applies for social networking. Being authentic in your relationships is the new way to do business. People want to be connected to others who actually care about them.

Build Your Community

I don't need to list culturally relevant ways for you to build your community; you know how to do that both in person and on the Web. This is just a final reminder to build your community with integrity. Use social networking sites with discernment. Don't become the guy who's e-mailing everyone from Facebook or LinkedIn. Be the person who is trying to serve others—this is the genesis for building a significant career. The art to building a lasting community is to go about it in every facet of your life. When you take your kids to soccer games or out to the park or to a professional sporting event, be aware of your surroundings. Not only do people watch how you treat and love your family, but there are also plenty of opportunities to pour into others. Who knows—your next great business relationship might surface on the sideline of your child's soccer game.

When you begin to build community in all areas of your life, you not only bring integrity to your work, but you also bring authenticity to your local environment. No one wants to be around a greedy networker. People want to be listened to; they want to matter.

When others begin to open up to you because they trust that you care, you are creating a new kind of success that has been buried in our culture for too long. Your business or career could plateau for the next ten years, and the only thing your neighbors might see is a person who seeks the greater good—a genuinely successful person. Successful because of the requisite BMW in the driveway? No. Successful because you value others above all. And that brings significance not only to your life but also to the lives of others.

If you dismiss the idea of pouring into others, you may still find success. But it's a transient success that will soon fade. And it's success you'll enjoy all alone. What good is it to gain the whole world but not have anyone to share your accomplishments with? Genuine significance—significance that lasts—comes from finding an outlet that allows you to lift others up, a place where you can pour yourself into others and a place where you can be an open book before others.

Then you're really someone who matters.

EIGHTH TENSION POINT

Getting Serious vs. Having Fun

> I had all the fun little creature comforts—a sweet car,
> motorcycle—and I was ready to buy a home in Arizona for an
> investment. I was set, and that's when the idea came to me.
>
> —John, businessman and world traveler

Success in your career requires sincerity, but if you're too serious, a job can become a burden. In order for your work and life to enhance each other, there must be a balance between professionalism and pleasure. The person who said you shouldn't mix business and pleasure was misled. This chapter will explain how business can be part of—and party to—life pleasure.

Careers are serious. Either we work our fingers to the bone pursuing the "dream job" or we educate our minds into oblivion hoping to supersede the race and land at the top. And for those of us in between, who are plugging away at our daily routine in order to support our families and have a small slice of the good life, careers are just as serious—if not more so.

Careers are fun. I've spoken with landscapers who are driven by the smell of fresh cut grass—guys who live for 5:00 a.m.—and think they've stumbled upon career nirvana. Then there's the used car salesman who lives for the auto auction. These guys are rolling the dice every week, looking for the perfect deal. It's a fast-paced career geared for a special breed; most guys I've talked to love it all.

Careers are a necessary evil. For every person I've spoken to who is either seriously invested in or flat-out excited about their job scenario, there are ten others in the gray zone. They are just putting in their time. Any career path they had an affinity for they left behind the slamming high school doors. A career to them is something they must do to support their standard of living. It is something everyone does. For them, it makes no difference if they take it seriously or have fun doing it; it's all about putting in the time. One day they hope to retire, but they're not sure how to get there. Life, career, family—these are all necessary, but each holds no promise of the future. They are what they are.

So which one are you? Are you all business in your career? Do you desire an element of fun in your job? I hope you're not drifting somewhere in the middle, indifferent to it all. My guess is that you picked this book up because you are interested in being someone who thinks tightrope walking through life is a better option than hanging on for dear life. You're the type who is dedicated to your job out of responsibility *and* affinity. You want to grow in your position and skill set. You like to have fun in life but are not sure how fun translates into your daily routine or into your career path in general.

In this chapter we will discuss the tension that exists between being responsible in your job and the need for levity to offset the seriousness of it—no one wants a job to become a burden. I'm sure many of you are saying, "But there's a reason they call it work. It's not supposed to be fun." We've certainly been pounded with that axiom enough. The truth is, there are plenty of studies that conclude having fun at work boosts productivity and company loyalty.

301 Ways to Have Fun at Work is a creative book based on the premise that most people are eager to take risks and give their loyalty to a company if the *experience* is enjoyable. The *Gallup Management Journal*

reported that "84% of highly engaged employees believe they can posi-
tively impact the quality of their organization's products, compared with
only 31% of the disengaged."[1] "Workers' Playtime," an article published
in *Journal of Applied Behavioral Science*, suggested that "organizations
should break with the conventional wisdom of delineating work from
play and instead craft an environment of fun and humor." And we're just
breaking the surface. The truth is out. If you want loyalty, productivity,
and strong mental health out of your employees, then you better engage
them with some good old-fashioned fun.

If we take a quick step back into ancient history, we find that work
was something man was designed for. The Judeo-Christian belief sys-
tem places Adam in the Garden of Eden with a mandate from God "to
work it and take care of it" (Genesis 2:15). What was obviously created as the archetype working relationship between mankind and God
was fractured when Adam and Eve did what they wanted, according
to their pride and greed. Because of their actions God said, "By the
sweat of your brow you will eat your food until you return to the
ground, since from it you were taken; for dust you are and to dust you
will return" (Genesis 3:19).

Mankind has toiled ever since. Over the course of time, work
became something degrading to the wealthy and was relegated to the
lower classes. What many people do not realize is that the Protestant
Reformation did more to change the ideas and approaches to work
than any other movement in world history. Martin Luther, perhaps the
most popular monk ever, preached that professional skills and gift sets
were things that could be used for the common good as well as to glorify God.

This paradigm shift introduced a new era of work. From what
today we would call the white-collar professional to the blue-collar
craftsman, all men and women were empowered to take pride in
their areas of labor. What used to be seen as degrading was held in

high esteem. People began to recognize the value of applying their skills and gifts to a task and seeing what they could produce. Eventually this led to the Industrial Revolution, which blew the doors of innovation and creativity wide open and changed the world of work forever.

What's the one thing that really excites you? Popular author, speaker, and creative guy Kevin Carol calls that one thing that gets you fired up more than anything else in life the "red rubber ball." He says, "Your red rubber ball is what grabs you by the soul. It's what captures your imagination. It's what you do when no one tells you what to do."[2] The world imagines a red rubber ball as nothing but a childhood toy. Kevin disagrees. The rubber ball is *the* thing you should pursue. It's what makes your work seem like play.

It is our task now to bring a healthy imbalance to the work/life tension that we all encounter. What tends to happen in society is that once mankind is empowered to do something, that empowerment plays out to the extreme. Though many draw significance and value from their work, it can infringe on our personal lives and rob us of the joy of our professions. It's time to right the ship.

Corporate Fun Starts in Little League

Think back to Little League baseball. It was all about fun. Once high school ball started, however, the stakes were higher—things were more serious. When athletes move into college sports, then it is yet another game. It becomes even more of a business when you hit college and your life revolves around studies and practice. But the sports programs that separate themselves from the rest are the ones with coaches who understand how to harmonize the business of the sport with fun. Without that harmony the sport becomes a drudge.

The same is true for businesses. People want to work for organizations that create an environment that balances the work of the day with the fun of the moment. The Great Place to Work Institute, a research and management-consulting firm, recently reported an upswing in growth among *Fortune* magazine's top 100 companies to work for over a seven-year period. The reason? They see the importance of fun at work.

Take Google, for example. CNN recently reported that Google is, once again, the number-one company to work for among Fortune 100 companies. Employees cite workplace flexibility within their jobs, all the quirky Google perks, and financial security among the top reasons to love Google. The top reason for the Google-love, however, is that they encourage their employees to dedicate 20 percent of their work-week to a project of their choice. This freedom creates a vibrant environment that makes the work exciting and fun for Googlers. Imagine the charge you would get knowing that you could chase your own Google dream one day each week. Now, that's fun.

While researching this chapter I ran across a blog by a staff writer at *Fast Company* magazine. He was opining about an industry event he had attended where the *Fast Company* CEO was imparting wisdom to the crowd. His nugget of advice? "Have fun, make sure your employees have fun, and make sure their families are having fun . . . No company ever went out of business while having fun. Work ceases to be fun long before that happens."

From Cisco to Starbucks, top companies understand that a fun work environment is key to attracting a talented work force. My Corporate Fun Award has to go to Yahoo! One of their core values is fun. "At five years of service employees get a gumball machine, at ten years an espresso machine, and at fifteen years (not possible until 2010) a foosball table." I'll take a gumball machine any day of the week!

These company approaches not only lighten up the workplace but also boost employee performance. More people are looking for jobs that provide more than a paycheck. People are looking for better work/life balance. More people are seeking social relevance in their work. The days of "doing time" at the workplace are slowly fading.[3]

No one knows this better than my friend, John. With success in his back pocket and a promising future, John wondered if there was more to a job than earning six figures and coping with stress. He found his answer on the other side of the planet.

Around the World

John's story begins with a drive many can relate to—ambition. Talented and smart, John had many opportunities in the corporate world but also found himself in his share of precarious positions. One of those positions was a nonprofit start-up that helped pay for basic needs of low-income children. As the acting vice president of sales and marketing as well as cofounder, John helped to build the company's success. The San Diego-based organization was going well. Right up until the point where other cofounders were being litigated. In the words of John's wife, "There's a big difference between looking good and being good." Lesson learned. Moving on.

The next opportunity for John seemed to be a perfect fit. It fulfilled him and excited him—it had a little bit of everything he liked. John never went into a new job blindly. From the outset of his career, he established a few key elements that he desired for his career.

"I've always tried to be intentional about staying away from corporate America," John said. "I've always had this list of things that I want to keep sacred. Things like heavy business travel I took seriously. Though I wasn't opposed to traveling altogether, I didn't want it to overtake my life."

John was a step ahead for having an idea of where he would and would not compromise in his job. He also sought passion in his work.

"Whatever I ended up doing for an extended period of time, I wanted it to be something I could really sink my teeth into."

So John took the job—a sales executive for a successful title company. It had all the perks: car allowance, great pay, and it gave John the opportunity to schmooze clients with premier tee times, dinners, and concerts. He had the ideal setup. Not only did the job offer him a significant amount of fun, but it was also demanding.

John enjoyed the relational side of the job, the outside-the-office part of it. But the stakes were high in this career, and it carried a correspondingly high amount of stress. It was a job he knew he would not be happy in for the rest of his life. Eventually it would become drudgery.

John recalled the time right before the idea hit him. "Everything was going well. I had money in the bank and a great place to live," he mused. "I had all the fun little creature comforts: a sweet car, motorcycle, and I was ready to buy a home in Arizona for an investment. I was set, and that's when the idea came to me."

John's big idea was taking a few months off—a year if it came to that—to travel around the world. He had the money. He was nearly indispensable at his job, yet his boss was okay with him leaving for an extended period of time, even promising to keep his job for him when he returned. It's hard to turn down an offer like that. So, he took it.

Traveling Is No Cakewalk

Everyone John talked to about his trip told him it was the chance of a lifetime. And it was. Most people go their whole lives dreaming of an epic trip like that, but for John this dream soon became a reality.

Admittedly a bit naïve heading into the preparations, John came to the realization that a trip around the world is not just as simple as hopping on several flights here and there. It takes planning and time and flexibility. Often our most memorable experiences are the ones that take us to our personal failing points—to the brink of who we are. For some it is a trip like John's; for others it turns out to be a more harrowing experience. In any case, the key point to realize when traversing through one of those life-changing experiences is to learn from the perspective offered by the experience.

To get a glimpse of John's life-changing experience, let's look at his abbreviated itinerary (in his own words):

John's Travel Journal

Entry 1: June 6, 2006. Today I left for my trip. I spent a week in New
    York City with my family—they saw me off to London. This was my
    first time outside of the U.S. other than Mexico and Canada.

Entry 2: Just landed in London . . . My plan is to contact a friend of
    mine who lives downtown. But before I could accomplish this I had a
    few questions alarmingly unanswered: How do I get into town? After
    I stay with this friend, where do I stay during the rest of the trip?
    How much money do I need? Then it hit me. The only idea I had of
    what to expect on this trip was from travel guides. This was not a
    normal vacation. I quickly realized I had to plan and think ahead.
    Though a bit daunting, I loved the challenge!

Entry 3: I figured out how to get to central London but didn't know
    where I was going to stay. I had to take a train to get something to
    eat. I tried to use my prepaid calling card to call a friend in London,
    and it took me forty-five minutes to get it to work. Small problem: I
    had not talked to my friend with the flat in London. Not sure what's
    going to happen. Calling card is not working out, so I dumped it and
    bought a prepaid cell phone. I finally got in touch with my friend, and
    we set up a meeting time that evening—it was morning, so I roamed
    around London all day.

Entry 4: During my wait I e-mailed everyone who was worried about me
    and let them know I had made it. There I was in the middle of the

business district with shorts, a sleeveless T-shirt, a backpack, and rolling bags. Question of the day: "Can somebody tell me what to do?"

Entry 5: Success! I arrived at my friend's flat and found an interesting sleeping scenario: a lesbian couple on the bottom bunk and my friend on the top bunk. Welcome to London!

Entry 6: My journey continues. Today I walked all of London and headed north to Scotland. But I missed the train to Ireland, so I went back to southwestern England through Wales to hop a boat to Ireland. Ireland is green! Now I'm on my way back to London and then straight to France. I hope to really take in Paris and am hoping I can make it down to the south of France to a castle my aunt lived in.

Entry 7: I borrowed my aunt's car and drove to Switzerland for a spell. After a few days there I went back to France, dropped the car, and headed to Barcelona. This is really cool: while checking out Barcelona I inadvertently met up with travelers I'd previously met in France, and we decided to travel in a small group for a while. My time with them was one of the best experiences of my entire trip.

Final Journal Entry: So, from France I made my way to Italy and then back to Switzerland. Once there I met up with a friend. We did a whirlwind stint and traveled to Sicily, Greece, and then to Germany, to Austria and Hungary, the Czech Republic, and back to Italy, then to Greece and Egypt. The end of my journey was nothing short of amazing. Each stop brought its own unique experience; each experience carried its own nugget of knowledge that I will forever hold.

John's Epiphany

"At this point I understood that traveling is work. What's more, I realized that traveling is a microcosm of my work/life tension. In order to survive on my epic journey I had to find purposeful imbalance. I had to enjoy the times of fun and wonder and the 'aha' moments while staying focused on my next move. I had to keep track of my upcoming destinations and make a plan for how to reach them. I had to budget my money and make sure I was going to places where my reserve funds were accessible if I needed more.

"My early naïveté met the reality of the moment with a bit of a thud at the beginning. But I eventually found my rhythm, and things began to fall into place. I had the time of my life."

The Epiphany of Harmony

Let's break down John's epiphany. But before we do that, allow me to recap the progression in John's story. First, John experiences some bumps along the career path as well as some welcome success. The success comes in a job that he is comfortable in and enjoys. The fun factor is there for him in that he is out of the office a good bit of the time and is able to be relational—something he is good at.

The only caveat to this scenario for John is that he cannot see himself continuing in this field for the long haul. In John's words it is not something he can "sink his teeth into."

The ideal situation for John would be a career that fuels his personal passion. This point is key and touches on some points made in previous chapters. When you pursue and land in a career path that not only matches your skill set but also fuels your passion, several things happen:

- Your work no longer feels like work—drudgery exits the building.
- Your work becomes enjoyable—road bumps turn into fun challenges.
- Your stress is minimized—with drudgery gone, stress feels completely different.
- Your workplace productivity is maximized.

John realized an important lesson at the beginning of his journey. He learned that even the best experiences in life—the ones yielding the most fun—were also laden with elements of responsibility and accountability. Translated: the best fun in life still requires an element of work.

So flip the coin. Shouldn't the same be true for work? Shouldn't the best job in life be rewarding and fun? Shouldn't every job that demands long hours and sacrifice have an inherent element of enjoyment? The answer is yes, but like everything else in life, you must be intentional about developing it.

John's trip was all-out fun but required a good bit of planning and a fair amount of responsibility. Some diligent work made things run smoothly, and he was able to enjoy his travels to the fullest. If you turn the tables of this scenario and apply it to your job, it might look like this:

Mr. X's Work/Life Log

Entry 1: I began my new job three months ago. All my friends were excited that I was able to find something so uniquely complementary to my passions and skill set.

Entry 2: Six months into it and I am realizing this job is demanding, though extremely rewarding. However, my days are getting longer and longer—I'm starting to feel overwhelmed.

Entry 3: My typical day: Wake up at 6:00 a.m. but skip my usual workout at the gym—clients are all wanting their product ASAP. After a quick Starbucks I'm at the office taking calls and answering e-mails for two hours. The rest of the day has me in meetings with potential clients, partners, and advertisers. By 7:00 p.m. I am heading out for Chinese food, picking up my dry cleaning, and crashing at my townhouse. I spend the next few hours answering more e-mails and working on a new proposal for our parent company. Then I hit the brick wall and fall asleep on the couch. I wake up at 2:00 a.m. and sleepwalk back to bed. Six o'clock comes very quickly—it all starts over.

Entry 4: I know I can't keep up this pace, so I consult a friend who gives me some great advice: "You need some fun in your life. What good is a jam-packed day and life if you can't take time to enjoy it? Plus, you look horrible."

Mr. X's Epiphany

"I realize that even though this job is rewarding on every level for me, fun is the harmonizing factor that keeps me purposefully imbalanced. My work environment is fast paced and extremely exciting, which for me is fun. I don't need games at work or anything like that—I just need some ease and adventure unrelated to my job peppered *into* my job.

"For this season I have to put in longer hours. But if I continue to go full throttle without a bit of levity, then I will burn out. So I've made some minor adjustments to my work environment and schedule to keep me tuned up and excited to go on."

Fun Tweaks to a Hard Day

- *Hire an Assistant.* I know not everyone has this luxury, but the friend who gave me the good advice runs a home business and she uses college students to help her with administrative things. It's not completely out of reach.

  My assistant filters my e-mails, picks up my dry cleaning, and even does Starbucks runs for us both. Adding her to my team makes complete sense. The pace of the day is better managed, and I have time for a morning workout—or for my newest hobby, rock climbing.

- *Flex Schedule.* After passing the idea by my superiors, I implemented a schedule that allows me to work from home two days a week. The benefits to this are obvious. Aside from the pay increase generated by not having to buy so much gas, I'm able to keep a low profile on Monday and Fridays.

This is huge for me. The office provides me with plenty of interruptions—at home I can get more accomplished because my time there is more concentrated. The by-products of this are that my work is done earlier and it allows me time for a new hobby.

- *Weekly Lunch with Friends.* Each week I plan a lunch with friends. We typically go somewhere different each time to keep things interesting. This one-hour lunch is a rejuvenating respite for us. We hear how each other's careers are going and are able to offer advice for those who are struggling or need encouraging. Our lunch lets us know we are not alone in this fast-paced life. Relationships are so important to me; usually they are the first things to go once careers get into full swing. I look forward to this hour each week.

Mr. X has successfully applied the lessons John learned on his trip around the world. His new career path was everything that he had hoped for in a job. It did not take him long, however, to realize that, though it's important to work hard at what you love, it can easily get the best of you. Offset that hard work with levity and times of fun can be part of your everyday life.

John's incredible trip around the word highlighted another truth that many people know but seldom apply. Extended times of fun can produce a profound perspective.

A Profound Perspective

"I realized, on my trip, that I'm not a one-job kind of guy," John explained. "The challenge of figuring out how to navigate new places and getting from point A to point B stirred something new in me. I told myself that when I returned home, it was time for me to strike out on my own—to see what would happen if I went independent."

It is easy to become locked into a particular way of doing things.

We seldom take the time to reevaluate our path. If you remember, Summer had the opportunity to step back because it was more or less forced upon her. But that time proved invaluable—she used it to incorporate significant improvement into her personal life and into her career path.

Similarly, John's trip around the world accomplished more than simply providing John with the time of his life—it alerted his mind and heart that he was built to be independent in his professional life.

Though not everyone can go on a trip around the world, the principle John brought back with him still applies. Adding fun to life provides us with a break from the monotony, from the serious business of life and work, and gives us—to use an athletic term—"fresh legs." Often we run through life as if it's a sprint—finish school, get that great job, get married, crank out the children—you get the picture. In the microcosm of a career, it's easy to put on the blinders and make a dash for the finish line, taking short breaks along the way.

But life is not a sprint. It's a marathon. Pace is key, and margin is its best friend. If you read magazines, you know all about pace. Editors use paragraph format and design to give the reader breaks in the action. Your eyes will read a few shorter paragraphs followed by a longer one more easily than an enormous paragraph jammed with all sorts of information.

Life and career need pace. Sprinting to the finish line will only beat you down and wear you out. Instead of driving yourself and your family into the ground and then breaking for a vacation just before you mentally collapse, why not factor pace into your schedule? Adding time for some fun and rejuvenation during your work life will help you fend off burnout. You will be able to go longer with short breaks that allow your mind to enjoy something unrelated to your work.

This approach also pays dividends in your personal life. Think about how tired you are after a long day at the office or in the field—or a long week of travel. When you finally get home, you don't want to do anything, talk to anyone, or think. You are spent. If you have a family, being brain-dead when you are home does not bode well for a healthy situation.

Understandably, we all go through seasons when we have no choice but to push through on a project. Long hours and weekends are par for the course then. But this must be the exception, not the rule.

The rule should make the "seasonal sprints" bearable. You should be able to look down the pike and say, "Well, I'm going to have to go hard at this project for two weeks. But after that, at least I have my normal schedule to look forward to." Too many of us cannot say that. Our normal schedule is chaos. It is not purposeful imbalance; it is pointlessness.

Interrupting our days and weeks with fun is key to pacing. Without it we will all be out-of-breath sprinters, struggling toward the finish line. Work/life harmony comes when we infuse our schedules with playtime. This intentional pacing will reward us with a fresh perspective in every facet of our lives—including work.

Here are a couple of rules to keep in mind.

Fun Rule #1: Have Fun on Purpose

We are so driven by our jobs that we're too serious about them. We forget what it feels like to have fun and relax. The first rule is intentionality. If we don't take it upon ourselves to incorporate times of fun and play on purpose throughout the day, then we run the risk of sprinting with blinders on.

On his trip around the world, John discovered that he had to be intentional about staying fiscally responsible, planning his itinerary, and navigating the journey. What John learned about serious responsibility in the midst of having the time of his life, we can apply to our daily routine of responsibilities and "serious" careers. In order to find a healthy harmony in either scenario, we must purposefully pursue one while simultaneously doing the other.

Harmony does not happen on its own. You must be intentional about offsetting the serious side of life with times of levity. Write the following on a sticky note and slap it on your laptop or dashboard: *Remember, have fun on purpose.*

Fun Rule #2: Have Serious Fun

No one wants a job that isn't taken seriously. Like John, we all want something we can sink our teeth into—something we're passionate about. Who are we if our primary cares in life revolve around facts and figures, shipping and receiving—the bottom line? We become one-dimensional. We lose that special something that makes people want to be around us.

Too many people accept the myth that being responsible means to be tight-fisted when it comes to fun. How absurd. The people who are performing dynamically for their companies are the ones who understand that the workday needs a bit of lightheartedness.

On the other hand, it is possible to care too much about fun and fail to take your work seriously. In John's account executive position he said he loved the mix of fun—the schmoozing of clients with golf outings and dinners—but also appreciated the serious nature of his work. It's important to honor the position you have with a sharp performance. When you are serious about your work, your performance will speak for itself. Others will honor your work ethic and be more accepting of your fun nature. A top performer who knows how to mix it up and let loose is different than a "performer" who is more show than substance.

Interpreting the Pyramid

This chapter has some similarities to the Sixth Tension Point and Summer's experiences. John's story is a journey toward the same principles that Summer has. They both reached a point of self-realization. John was searching for a job he could enjoy— one that would challenge him, develop his passions, and stoke his inner fires for fun. John's trip provided the needed experience to allow him to see what he needed to strive for.

Because John had worked hard to get to the place where he could take time off for something he had always wanted to do, he was able to broaden his life experience. By pushing himself into an experience that was largely unfamiliar and unknown, he discovered things he didn't know about himself—like the fact that he felt it was time to be independent in his career.

When you are constantly pushing hard in a demanding and serious career, it's easy to become blinded by the immediate. For John, some good old-fashioned fun and time away was just what the doctor ordered. Having fun and letting loose led to a self-realization that empowered his next career move.

Now, as John seeks out his independence in the professional world, he will be operating from the focal point of self-realization. His decisions hereafter will not be based primarily on human needs or esteem-building issues. He will be free to seek out a career path that not only meets his needs but one that will benefit others. This is the major differentiator in approaching career development with Maslow's pyramid inverted.

This perspective cannot be overstated. When we finally realize what makes us tick, our career decisions become more outwardly

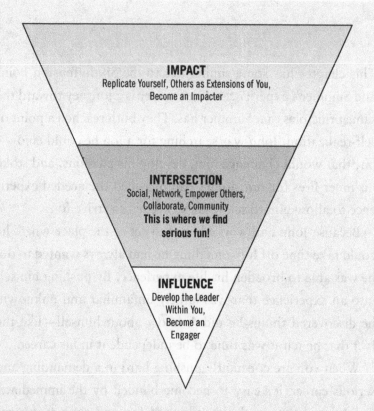

focused. We are more confident making a decision to pursue the dream that was always tucked away in our hearts. We feel empowered to do something that matters in the grand scheme of life—something that gives back to the community. And when we can give of ourselves in our professional lives, our personal lives become more vibrant. The human needs are no longer the drivers in our professional decisions; now they are secondary, which allows us to experience a greater sense of being.

Striving for harmony is a tender endeavor. No one ever said it was going to be easy to pull off. It requires a fair amount of risk—walking forward on the tightrope. But the progress we make is all the more rewarding when it includes a serious bit of fun.

Working Hard vs. Staying Healthy

In business, in fitness, and in everything else in life, consistency is
more important than perfection.

—Bill, Ironman Triathlon competitor

Numerous studies indicate that poor health is rampant in the
workplace. Is it any wonder? With long hours, tough competition, and rigid expectations, the body and mind are under constant
stress. This leads to low productivity on the job, less energy off the
job, and a shortened lifespan. But culture shows no signs of slowing;
you either adapt or get smothered. There is no in-between.

As culture speeds up, the lines between workplace and home become
blurred, leaving very little space to unplug from the work environment. Even Microsoft founder Bill Gates is not immune; he admitted
that the lines between work and home are fuzzy. "People used to go to
work at a specific time, come home, and have white space in their lives
during commutes or other times," he said. "Now you can impose upon
yourself a never-ending flood of information."[1]

This constant information stream leaves you feeling cornered and
agitated, which translates poorly into family life. Clocking out at the
end of the day has been replaced by the BlackBerry and iPhone that keep

141

the information flowing. So now, even when you're at home trying to enjoy your family, you're fair game to clients and the boss.

As the tyranny of the immediate begins to dictate your life, you slowly begin to drop things that used to keep you fresh and sane. You cancel your gym membership, unload your new cyclocross bike on Craigslist, and that once-a-quarter camping trip you once took with friends up north is no more. All in the name of progress.

There may not be a wrong or right answer to this cultural problem. We cannot become isolated monks if we are seeking influence in our careers. On the other hand, we can't expect to maintain a full family life and a rewarding personal experience if we give in to the demands of our fast-paced culture.

Many of us who are tethered to our BlackBerries and laptops yearn for that time on the treadmill or in the lap pool or on the mountainside. We need that time to unwind and allow the lactic acid to sweat out of us. But we realize we've let all that slip. Far from being harmonious, the work/life relationship is a dissonant chord striking over and over again in our minds, breaking our backs with guilt. We know we should be getting our exercise—we know we should be getting outside, but we can't bring ourselves to leave the rat race behind even for an hour.

We are slaves to our drive to achieve more and be more. The irony is that the more we strive for professional success without a focus on our personal health, the more we rob those dear to us of a person who has the drive to earn the huge bonus and the energy to spend it on a fun trip to the Grand Canyon—or something like that.

In his poem "The Best Medicines," Henry Wadsworth Longfellow declared, "Joy and Temperance and Repose/Slam the door on the doctor's nose." I love his use of the words *joy* and *repose*. If only we could weave these two ideas into our personal life, then we would be well on our way to healthy living, not to mention a professional career that thrives.

In this chapter we'll look at how to remain diligent at work while simultaneously maintaining a healthy, enduring lifestyle. To help shed some light on the topic, I contacted my friend Bill Bachrach, CEO and Ironman. His story and insights are invaluable. Not only is he an inspiration to me professionally, but his commitment to a healthy lifestyle is contagious. Anyone who tackles the Hawaiian Triathlon in order to get into shape has my full attention. I hope you catch a little of Bill by reading this chapter.

Choose or Lose

We have become professional packagers. We package away segments of our lives into neat little spaces. Over here we have our professional package. We manage it with a certain set of rules and boundaries. Over here, next to the Twinkie, is our personal life. We wrap it in its own special packaging—it is managed differently than our personal life. Some of us even package our religion or faith experience in a separate space as well. None of them touch; each is managed separately; all is nice and neat. Right?

I hope the previous paragraph does not describe you. But if it does, I would suggest that it's time for a new perspective. When I hooked up with Bill to discuss this chapter, the first question I asked him was, "How does your personal life feed off of your professional life?"

He responded, "Well, first of all, I choose big goals, personally and professionally. My mantra is to do interesting things with interesting people. My personal and professional life definitely feed off each other. Perhaps the most important aspect of that is my personal choice to be healthy and fit."

He continued, "My personal and professional lives are interrelated. Not because I work on vacation or think about vacation when I'm at work, but because I need to have enough money to have the freedom to do the things I want to do outside of work." For Bill, all of life—personal and professional—is connected. This mind-set has allowed him not only to succeed professionally but also to find significance in his personal life as well.

"Many of the things I enjoy don't require much money, but they do require freedom. And some of the things I want to do outside of work, like fund philanthropic endeavors, could require lots of money. Professional success affords me the economic means and the freedom to pursue the other things that matter to me in life. Physical success makes it all possible. These are the equivalent of air and water to life."

Bill dismissed the notion that a segmented or prepackaged life is an option for harmonic living. "Obviously, you can't achieve big goals if you feel bad," he went on. "And even if you don't feel bad, you almost certainly need to feel your best to do your best. I think choosing to be fit and healthy is just that, a choice."

Bill has a way of simplifying the seemingly difficult or complex things in life. When he mentioned that a fit and healthy life was a choice, he became emphatic:

Being successful in business is a choice.
Being good at your job is a choice.
Being committed to your spouse is a choice.
Being a committed parent, brother, sister is a choice.
It's your choice. And being fit and healthy will almost certainly affect every other choice in your life in a positive way. Aligning your behavior with some choices is easier than others, but it's all still a choice.

Yet even if we finally realize and admit that being fit is a choice, the decision to pursue fitness does not automatically become easy. There is a reason behind every choice we make. Bill said, "If the reasons are big enough, then following through with the behavior that supports the choice is easier. Notice I didn't say 'easy.' I said '*easier*.'"

One of the first things we should do is answer this question: *What are the reasons behind the current choices I am making professionally and personally?*

Chances are your reasons for doing the things you do professionally are directly related to financial success and hierarchical power. If you continue down a certain path for a few more years, you will be set financially; or if you do not put in the hours the other guys are putting in, then you will be passed over for the promotion. These reasons all seem great and lofty at the moment we make them. But when we look back and see what those decisions have cost us in our personal lives, things do not look so peachy.

It is time to make some choices—some tough choices. It is time to evaluate and decide to pursue health as part of your recipe for success. It is time to realize that when we seek out personal health and fitness, we extend deeper significance to our lives. We are not just power-mongers or machines bent on making a buck. We are live human beings who realize that life harmony exists, not necessarily in a mystical or ethereal way, but in a way that brings a healthy imbalance to our professional life.

When our bodies are nurtured, our minds will follow. And a decision to cultivate both is the first step toward personal fulfillment.

But I Always Fail at Workouts

No doubt many of you reading this have attempted to get into better shape before and failed. You have purchased thousands of dollars worth of equipment, tried crazy diets, or even gone to a boot camp. You do not want to live with the guilt of trying and failing. Fine. Understood. But do not let guilt dictate your health.

Bill touched on this point in our conversation; he dealt with the same issue. "Forgiveness," he said, "is very important. Recognizing that you can't change history is important. So, when I have a bad exercise day or week or month, I don't beat myself up about it. All I can do is use the past to motivate me to have a better present and future."

We all have bad days, even bad weeks. Many of us have great intentions, but when the holidays hit, football and apple pie win out. Jordan S. Rubin, author of *The Maker's Diet*, said that you are only one meal away from eating healthy. The same principle applies here. We all blow it. Forgive yourself and move on.

Bill agreed. "When I have a bad exercise day, I vow to make tomorrow a good exercise day. When I have a good exercise day, I vow to do the same on my next scheduled exercise day."

If you have to resort to getting creative with your workouts, do it. Bill likes to use a training log to make a game out of getting healthy. Just as in business, there are ways to measure your progress as you become more fit. A training log can be your spreadsheet, a record of your ups and downs, your milestones and setbacks. You will be surprised how the simple act of writing down your progress will encourage you to keep after it.

Bill said, "For me, turning my workout regimen into something fun helps me stay excited about it. It helps me stay sharp, mentally and physically, for the other important things in my life. I have a cycling routine that I flat-out love. I do it because it's fun and it helps me keep my life and goals in perspective."

Bill does not allow outside influences to dictate why he rides his bike to keep in shape. His workouts are like mini-vacations for him. He lets them enrich his life rather than being drudgery or something high pressure that is added to his schedule.

Your workouts should be fun. This will help you get rid of that guilty feeling when you don't stay with your routine. When you miss, it won't be something you beat yourself up over. It will be something you can't wait to get back to.

My discussion with Bill carried over into e-mail. I am sharing two e-mails that stayed with me as I thought through this chapter. Bill dispelled some common myths about what it takes to stay healthy while being successful at work. Here are those e-mails, along with a few of my own insights.

Myth #1: Exercise Will Hinder My Productivity

(Truth: Iron man, iron business!)

Todd: If you're like me, you are driven in your work. You love what you do so much that it's tough to pull yourself away and keep that healthy imbalance of working hard and playing hard. If you're like me, then you too deal with the misconception that a workout regimen will hinder your productivity on the job. This could not be further from the truth.

Bill: I know exactly what you're talking about, Todd. From age twenty-nine to thirty-seven I was building a new business and struggled to squeeze in an average of just two thirty-minute jogs each week. Sometimes I would go weeks without exercising. I rationalized that it was impossible for me to do that and still build my business.

Bingo! Bill hit the nail on the head.

At some point we all deal with this notion. Success in work and in life, however, demands that as we push to achieve, we stay healthy and fit. How many guys or gals do you know who have gained weight and allowed their health to deteriorate in the name of professional success? It simply is not true: you don't have to sacrifice your health to keep your career going.

Bill: In hindsight, I'm sure my business actually grew more slowly because of my lack of exercise. I worked long hours, but I believe they were less effective and less productive than they would have been if I had been exercising more.

Bill was asserting the perspective of wholeness. We often view exercise as a distraction, but the truth is it makes us more of a whole person.

Pierre de Coubertin, the French educator who was instrumental in reviving the Olympic Games in 1894, said, "Olympism . . . [is] exalting and combining in a balanced whole the qualities of body, mind and will." De Coubertin made a keen insight. Many times our problems with exercise are that we view it as something separate from our "other life" as a professional. Instead we should view it as part of the whole picture that makes us who we are.

For Bill, discovering this kind of wholeness was a journey that took him through the rigors of training and participating in an Ironman Triathlon. Here is Bill's inspiring story:

When I was thirty-seven I had a unique opportunity to participate in the Hawaii Ironman Triathlon. *If* I could transform myself from a twice-a-week jogger into a person who could complete a 2.4-mile ocean swim, a 112-mile bike ride, and a 26.2-mile marathon run. And I had to do this transformation in ten months.

Completing the Hawaii Ironman had an interesting effect on my overall point of view that has made an impact on everything else in my life, personally and professionally. First of all, I wasn't sure I could do it. But I did. And that has forever changed my belief about what's possible in all areas of my life. Second, it made me realize that I could have been exercising at a reasonable level all along. After all, if I could grow my business while training for Ironman, I certainly could have fit in a few hours of exercise into my calendar all those previous years.

I have a successful training company for financial advisors. I never thought that a personal achievement would have an impact on my business. I was doing physical training for the Hawaii Ironman purely as a self-indulgence: to get myself in super condition and to enjoy the sense of accomplishment. I thought my business might suffer a little, but I couldn't pass up the opportunity to do something so cool.

Even if I didn't finish the race, I would still be better off. But a funny thing happened—my professional credibility went up. Financial advisors realized that I wasn't just someone teaching them what to do, how to overcome obstacles, and accomplish more in their businesses. I was someone who was willing to embrace a challenge and do the same thing in my life.

I have had many people tell me that hearing my story inspired them to figure out how to make health and fitness a part of their lives. One gentleman with a growing family and a growing financial services business told me at my last Academy that he completed his first Ironman distance triathlon. You don't have to do an Ironman, but it does beg the question, "What's possible for you?"

The bottom line is that you have time to exercise, eat well, and be good on the job. You just have to make it a priority. We all have 168 hours a week; how we choose to spend or invest those areas determines our success and quality of life.

If I want to be healthier but am worried that the time requirement will damage my professional life, how or where should I begin? It all starts with one small step at a time. Do something now; take the first step.

Myth #2: If I Miss a Day, I Have Failed

(Truth: Consistency is king!)

When I asked Bill how he managed the tension between working hard and staying healthy, he said that he didn't experience much tension between the two. In a vintage Bill retort he said, "I think the stress from working hard might be killing me prematurely. Running a business is hard work." Very true! Thanks, Bill.

There was no tension between working hard and staying healthy because Bill did not feel a huge need to be perfect in his workout regimen. Where others may beat themselves up or even give up if they miss a day, Bill saw it as an opportunity to start fresh the next day. Because he held working hard and staying healthy loosely, he felt the freedom to go after each with equal abandon.

But as in most things in life, it's not how perfect you are at something, it's how diligently you apply yourself to a task. Bill went on, "That's why I work at exercising consistently and eating well consistently. Notice I said 'consistently' not 'perfectly.' In business, in fitness, and everything else in life, consistency is more important than perfection."

So many people simply give up when they miss a week. They convince themselves that they're never going to be able to keep at it long enough for it to work, so they give up entirely. This is horrible self-talk and, basically, an outright lie. You do not need to be an athlete in training; you simply need to make a pact with yourself to stay healthy no matter what and do your best to keep after it.

Sure, life happens. You will miss a few days. You may even miss an entire week. So what? Learn from your life experience and do a better job at making space for your workout. It's up to you whether you need to train for a race or some kind of event to motivate yourself. But don't feel you have to. It's enough just to be consistent at your local gym or on your bike or on the running trail. The key thing is that you are out there doing it. Nike has the right idea—"Just do it."

Check out what Bill told me in an e-mail about consistency. Here's his take:

Dear Todd,

I was thinking about our conversation about being consistent when it comes to being healthy. Here is another thought that popped into my head after our conversation.

My favorite restaurant is In-N-Out Burger. If I were on death row, my last meal would be three Double-Doubles, fries, and a chocolate shake. I'd fight for a stay of execution just so I could do that twice. My second favorite food is pizza. And those little meat tacos from Taco Bell are fabulous! But, obviously, I can't eat that junk all the time.

One of the best ideas I have ever heard about eating well is that only nineteen of your twenty-one weekly meals need to be healthy. And that's pretty much how I approach eating well. If I can eat well nineteen of twenty-one meals a week, then I can really enjoy my two lousy meals a week without remorse or guilt.

Same for snacks. If most of your snacks are healthy (apple, carrot sticks, celery, yogurt, carrot juice, etc.), then an occasional candy bar isn't going to ruin your program.

Anyway, the point here is (obviously) trying to keep a consistent regime but leaving room in your life to enjoy things—like junky tacos. You don't have to be a health-food psycho to be a healthy eater. You just need to have a consistent plan of action.

Hope this helps the discussion!

Sincerely,

Bill

Bill's letter rings true to purposeful imbalance. Over and over Bill mentioned consistency. This is a key insight into our discussion about life/work harmony. Remember, purposeful imbalance is different than blatant imbalance. An imbalanced approach to staying healthy says, "All or nothing." The result is a guilty conscience due to continued failure. When we live our lives in reaction to something, we do not seek a healthy tension. Instead we swing from one extreme to another—a recipe for failure. In life this approach would throw us from the tightrope. Finding that harmony is key to maintaining a healthy life on the wire.

Based on my conversation with Bill, here are three keys for keeping a consistent approach to your exercise regimen:

1. *Set Goals.* It's easy to become overwhelmed with a workout regime unless you have a clear vision of what you wish to accomplish. Whether it's free weights, running, cycling, or rock climbing, be sure to set achievement marks for yourself. If you have something to work toward, you'll be less likely to make excuses for missing workouts. You will be more focused and anticipate great workouts instead of dreading the time. Achieving your goal will give you a sense of pride and accomplishment—a perfect recipe for keeping your professional fires stoked as well.

2. *Have Fun.* Perhaps I should have made this the number one key. It is paramount that you enjoy your workout time. But having fun is not just about sitting on the rowing machine with a huge grin on your face. It's about maintaining levity in your approach. Bill mentioned his love for In-N-Out Burger. Maybe you simply love Five Guys' French fries. Whatever it is, be sure to allow yourself the pleasure of "the good stuff" in life.

3. *Buddy Up.* Get a workout partner—find new friends at work. There are already people in your workplace who are exercising while succeeding professionally. Find out who they are and join them. Personal accountability is essential to many aspects in life, and working out is no different. Find someone who will take things seriously with you. Don't partner up with a guy or gal who is just in it to chitchat on the treadmill. Find someone who will push you when you are doing laps in the pool or maxing out on the bench press. A good workout partner could be the difference between a consistent and fun exercise session and a loathsome time at the gym with nothing but your iPod to keep you company.

Most communities have gyms, running groups, riding groups, martial arts classes, yoga, Pilates, and other places where healthy and successful people get together. They're always welcoming to newcomers who want to get involved in the activities they love. For example, the local bike shop will know the groups of other riders at your level. The local triathlon club will have a path for new triathletes.

Here's one last word of practical advice for keeping your workouts consistent. It's tempting to use business trips as excuses for not being able to keep your exercise program going. Bill told me about Peter Vidmar, a former Olympian. Peter was the captain of the 1984 U.S. men's gymnastics team. They won the first ever team gold medal at the Los Angeles Olympic Games. Peter also won the gold on the pommel horse and took the silver medal in the men's all-around.

Peter travels a lot as a speaker. Bill said, "When I told him I was training for Ironman, I asked for his advice. He gave me the secret to keeping fit on the road . . . Here it is, advice from an Olympic champion! After you check into your hotel room, don't turn on the TV until you get to the hotel gym. Brilliant! Simply brilliant."

Do not let any excuse keep you from meeting your goals and staying healthy. Peter's approach to exercise while traveling is also a great idea in the home. Put a piece of exercise equipment in front of your TV; sell your couch if you have to. Being fit and healthy is your choice. Choose wisely.

Aim Small, Miss Small

Keeping a healthy tension between a successful career and a healthy lifestyle doesn't happen on its own; you must be laser focused on it as a goal. When I think of focus, I think of taking aim at a target. In target shooting everyone knows to aim for the target. But the bigger question is not what you aim for, but how you aim.

In the film *The Patriot*, Mel Gibson's character is going after the British soldiers who took his oldest son after killing his second oldest son. He takes the two remaining sons with him as his sharpshooters. As they prepare their ambush in the woods, Mel reminds the boys, "Remember what I told you about shooting?" The boys answer, "Aim small, miss small." Mel replies with affirmation, "Aim small, miss small."

To be frank, I did not understand that advice right away. I had to think about it. After all, I am not a hunter or a target shooter. But after giving it some thought, it made perfect sense.

As you are picking what to aim for on the target, you are setting the parameters for what is possible for you to hit. If you're aiming at a typical target with a bull's-eye in red and you aim for the surrounding area of yellow, then you will most likely hit something within those parameters—maybe. It is not a very focused shot if you are aiming at a large target.

However, if you take aim directly at the bull's-eye—a very specific and small area—then you have a better chance of hitting on or near the bull's-eye. By aiming small you diminish your chances of hitting outside the bull's-eye area. But if you do miss the bull's-eye, chances are you will hit somewhere close.

So, if you aim small—aiming at the bull's-eye—you will miss small; you will hit somewhere near the bull's-eye. The point is that you must have laser focus in order to cultivate a healthy lifestyle while staying driven as a professional. A great example of laser focus relating to health issues is the TV show *The Biggest Loser*.

The show's recent success is an indicator that people are not simply lacking a healthy work/life tension but, in fact, have surrendered to the lie that says, "I can't keep a healthy balance of work or parenting in my life." America as a whole struggles more than any other country with obesity as well as depression—two clear signals that scream out: success or being a good parent is more important than staying healthy, and I can't do both.

In a recent interview on the *Today* show, Jillian Michaels, *The Biggest*

Loser's trainer, commented that women in particular struggle with "putting themselves first." Jillian observed that most women think that they must sacrifice their own well-being to be a good mother and housewife. But that simply is not the case. As Jillian pointed out, when women let their bodies become overweight and overrun with stress, they actually rob their families of their most precious gift—themselves.

In the interview Jillian gave some helpful tips for women just getting started on the road toward health:

- Keep your health first by getting enough sleep and eating healthy foods—when you do, other parts of your life will flourish.
- Learn to say no. Most people are spread too thin and simply allow their lives to become overrun with stress. Learn to value your yes. Do not kowtow to the worthless emotion of guilt.
- Find time to escape the family cycle. Familiarity breeds contempt, so do your best to get away to refuel. Whether it's a romantic retreat with your spouse or an overnight stay at a bed-and-breakfast alone, find time to refuel.
- Rediscover who you are. Take some time to reflect and identify the things that make you, you.

The show's success is due to the participants and their great stories. They become focused on getting healthy. They pick a goal and go after it with everything they have. These people are revolutionizing their lives with their single-minded determination to lose weight. We can pull two important lessons from this show.

First, resolve to correct bad life habits that cause you to lose focus and become a stranger to yourself and those who love you. If you're off the deep end in your work—you work incessantly, you are always stressed, your family is falling apart, and your health is becoming an issue—then you need to take hold and correct things. Evaluate your professional life and make serious concessions to regain a purposeful imbalance in your life.

Remember the inverted pyramid. If you are running so hard after success that your personal life is in shambles, then you are not even on the pyramid grid. The idea is to work from a place of self-knowledge, not self-destruction. A healthy you is someone who has the energy and well-being to help others rise to the place where you are. As you encounter people in your job and in your community, they should see someone who is confident, fit, and engaging. No one wants to be around or emulate an overweight, self-centered person—even a successful one—who inspires others to turn and run.

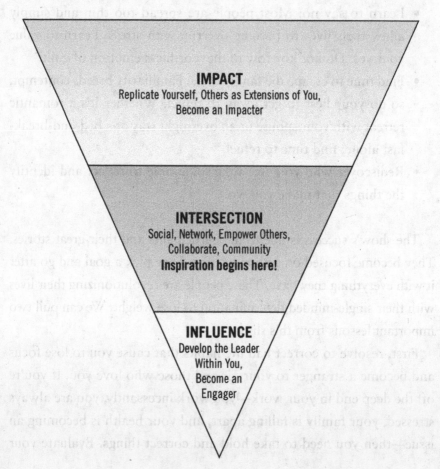

IMPACT
Replicate Yourself, Others as Extensions of You,
Become an Impacter

INTERSECTION
Social, Network, Empower Others,
Collaborate, Community
Inspiration begins here!

INFLUENCE
Develop the Leader
Within You,
Become an
Engager

People want to be inspired to reach for something that seems out of reach but is attainable with a bit of hard work. In order for you to be that person to others, you must correct the ship—you must regain your life harmony and leverage your ability to succeed professionally with your physical need to be healthy.

The second lesson we can learn from *The Biggest Loser* is the contestants' laser focus. It is truly inspiring to see someone achieve a goal they've worked really hard at. When you see the effect the show has on the lives of the contestants, it makes you want to be a better person, to work to achieve that which you know may be hard but is still within reach. Aim small, miss small.

If we as professionals—and as moms and dads and husbands and wives—can apply this level of focus to keeping healthy yet focused lifestyles, then we are winners. Our families and friends also reap the rewards of someone who is fit in mind, body, and soul.

A Repose

I want to take a minute to talk about one final aspect of staying healthy: rest. Our culture is so fast-paced that not resting is often a foregone conclusion. We simply do not rest. But the benefits of rest are immeasurable. A friend of mine who is an avid mountain biker often talks about getting the right amount of rest before and after rides. You will not find a serious athlete who never stops training. Rest is mandatory for peak performance. The same principle is true in our professional and personal lives. It is as important as jogging or cycling, but we seldom treat it as such.

In an article on creating "rest stops" in life, Gordon MacDonald said, "The benefits to genuine rest are clear. If there is a new sense of strength, an unusual vitality of mind, a set of balanced emotions, a greater sensitivity to right and wrong, we assume that there's been some rest behind it."[2]

But how can we rest when we are tethered to our BlackBerries and iPhones and laptops? As we've noted repeatedly, the lines of work and rest today are blurred, especially for those of us who are business owners or entrepreneurs. We are always on. Where is the point when I am no longer thinking of another idea for a book or solving a business problem in my head? When I meet with colleagues for a drink, we invariably talk shop. Is this rest or work?

Gordon MacDonald addressed this issue in his article citing a biblical solution to our cultural problem of not resting. "When God defined rest in the Scriptural teaching on the Sabbath he was quite clear: Six days you shall labor, but on the seventh day you shall do no work." With this definition of what it means to take a break—or a Sabbath rest—MacDonald concluded, "I have taken the discipline of rest rather seriously. The Sabbath is increasingly important to me: a day in which *income-producing work* is laid aside and a new 'work' is taken up. The work of renewing my marriage, my friendships, my relationship to God."

I know what some of you are thinking. *Whoa, that's too hard a line for me to take.* I would challenge you that the idea of a Sabbath rest of some kind is vital to your professional success. No one wants to be around you when you are irritable, stressed, overworked, and despondent. You are a detriment to yourself, your company, and to others. Sure you can string it along for some time. But you will crash eventually, and when you do, you will look back and wish that you had taken some time to breathe, away from the e-mails and conference calls.

But even more, you need to be rested so you can be present in your personal life. You need a personal life outside of your professional one. You need to be present for your wife or husband—that relationship does not run well on fumes. You need to fuel it with your whole being, not just your leftovers. You need to be present for your children, who are counting on you for moral support and for love and care—and don't forget fun too. Do not be a mom your kids keep away from. Do not be a dad who wonders why all the kids like to hang out at the Smith's house because the dad is so cool—it's because he plays with them.

Instead, be the man or woman who is vibrant on his or her "day off." The one who takes the kids on field trips and to ball games. Your children don't care that you are up for promotion or that you are the leading sales representative. They care whether or not you are present in their lives. Don't miss out. Take a day of rest—for you, for your family. When you do, you will understand that significance at work has less to do with being the best and more to do with the health of your mind, body, and soul.

Making Your Mark vs. Leaving a Legacy

Success requires living now, and significance requires lasting forever. If you want to make your life matter, then consider this: you must invest your work hours in something that will be legacy-leaving.

—Todd Duncan

What makes great leaders? Do we measure their success by the size of the organizations they leave behind or the bottom lines they build? Maybe. History shows leaders as they are in light of their accomplishments—but true leadership is measured with more than mere productivity. As observers, we see that the leaders who truly leave marks of success are the ones who carved out the intangibles, that certain something that elevates them above others. This is legacy.

Legacy is different from success. It is a body of work that, when held up to the light of reality, gives the student guidance and inspiration. It is the connection between successful numbers and moral triumph—it is a record of all that makes us who we are.

To put it plainly, it is the small-town print shop that becomes synonymous with quality work delivered on time. Everyone in town knows the print shop because the owners sponsor community events, support the local high school programs, and donate their resources for the betterment of the community. This is legacy defined in the positive. But there is a flip side.

In many ways, everyone leaves a legacy. It is just a matter of the kind of legacy left behind. The man who spends his time on the couch watching television all night after work shows his kids what it means to be an adult—in the negative sense. The corporate mogul who cuts corners to inflate the bottom line may produce high numbers, and this is his mark in life. But his legacy is shrouded in deception and selfish gain. He doesn't leave much of a legacy to be followed, but he still leaves one.

Each of us must ask, *What legacy am I leaving behind?* We are in the here and now, stamping life with our work, our passions, and our dreams. Each day we lift our heads off our pillows is a day we lay another brick in the foundation of our legacies. The marks we leave now become our legacies then.

There's a great quote from the movie *Shadowlands*, the story of C. S. Lewis' relationship with Joy Davidson. The famous quote from the film comes from Lewis as he reminisces of his time with Joy:

"Why love if losing hurts so much? I have no answers anymore. Only the life I have lived. Twice in that life I've been given the choice: as a boy and as a man. The boy chose safety, the man chooses suffering. The pain now is part of the happiness then. That's the deal."

"The pain now is part of the happiness then." He was speaking of the wonderful times spent with his wife, Joy, in the days before she lost her life to cancer. They both knew she didn't have much time left. They spent her last days enjoying their love. These times together accumulated as life marks—collecting in the future. They knew that the day would come when, as death approached, the times of love shared in the past would contribute to their pain in the now. This is what legacy does.

Legacy is the accumulated efforts and accomplishments of our lives.

But more, it is the motive that drives those accomplishments. Why did we push that project through? Why did we set that financial goal? Was if it for something greater than ourselves? Maybe we can say it as Lewis did. The impetus behind our accomplishments now is part of our legacies then.

Daily Legacy

Each day is full of problems, victories, and caffeine headaches. But what most people call "the grind" is really an opportunity—an opportunity to write another chapter of your legacy. The daily happenings spread out over time and become your life marks. These are the rather menial and obligatory tasks that define your days, weeks, and months. But hidden in the obligatory tasks are the treasures of legacy, the building blocks of what will be, wrapped up in the now.

If you are constantly looking for the next big break, you will ignore the present passing before you. It is in the now that legacy is built. Each small victory throughout life equals your accumulated legacy. It just doesn't happen from nothing, or all at once.

In today's world we see successful people on television or hear them on the radio and want to be like them. But we want it immediately, not realizing that most leaders who find national success do so only after decades and decades of hard work. At some point leaders in the limelight of culture have paid their dues and then some. Sleepless nights and untold failures dot the careers of many of the most recognized figures on the national scene. The average person is not willing to sacrifice so much for success.

Michael Jordan

Michael Jordan is an excellent example of a leader who was shaped by a life that had its fair share of pitfalls. Many young boys and girls watched

Michael play basketball, bought his jersey and his famous shoes, and even stuck out their tongue doing lay-ups—but few are willing to give themselves over to the sport as Michael did. We, as a culture, love to see the success of the few but fail to realize that success comes in the daily pursuit of excellence. But it wasn't just this pursuit that made Michael who he is. It was also his failures.

Nike ran a series of ads some time ago with MJ narrating. The short commercials highlighted what it means to become legendary—to produce a legacy. The script reads:

> I've missed more than nine thousand shots in my career. I've lost almost three hundred games. Twenty-six times I've been trusted to take the game winning shot—and missed. I have failed over and over and over again in my life. And that is why . . . I succeed.

Michael Jordan did not wake up one morning and decide to become the greatest basketball player of all time. He had a dream and pursued it with everything he had. He left nothing on the table. He could have given up when he was cut from his junior high basketball team, but he used it to fuel his passion instead.

How many of us accept defeat like that? Most times we simply allow it to point us into another direction. We ping-pong different interests until we fall into something that is comfortable—something that "fits" us. Success is not built overnight or instantaneously. It is being built constantly.

Lance Armstrong

Perhaps you are familiar with another athlete—a former cancer patient—who beat death to become the greatest cyclist ever. Lance Armstrong's rise to greatness came to the masses each July for seven straight years. For a month we followed him through mountain ranges and past villas and ultimately first across the finish line in the Tour de France.

But what we did not see were the grueling days between the races when Lance beat, honed, and prepared his body. We did not witness the agony of six hours of daily bike riding. None of us saw Lance forgo the creature comforts at his fingertips for a life of rigorous discipline. And certainly none of us were with him during his bout with testicular cancer.

Lance's story is so significant because he triumphed through major personal challenges and translated them into greatness doing the one thing he loves most of all: riding his bike. Lance's legacy was more than just endless hours of gut-wrenching training and cancer treatments. It was more than a decade of dedication to a particular calling on his life. A legacy must begin in anonymity before it is translated to the masses.

Walt Disney

Have you ever heard of Laugh-O-Gram Studios? Probably not. It's the name of Walt Disney's first animation studio, which went bankrupt in a year because of Walt's poor money management. A few years later Disney was forced out of the company that owned exclusive rights to his most popular character to date, Oswald the Lucky Rabbit. His replacement for Oswald? A mouse named Mortimer, inspired by the rodent that scampered around his office. At his wife's suggestion, he changed the name to Mickey Mouse. (In a Hollywood happy ending, Disney studios finally got the rights to Oswald in 2006.)

I hope you are beginning to see a trend here with some of the most inspiring legacies in our culture. Sure, sometimes greatness is born. But most often the people who leave legacies that change the world do so after countless failures and decades of hard work.

On a personal level, as we move through life we collect the experiences that testify to our personal success. And finally, when we look back and survey our success, we see that we hold more than a life basket of experience. We have accumulated a legacy. It is full of the years, failures, and victories past.

A Significant Investment

Legacy is accumulated over time. It is intentional living through everything life throws at you. Through the testing comes success. Legacy can be both negative and positive; it can be substantive, or it can be forgettable. So what sets a legacy of worth apart from an empty one? Significance.

Great leaders seek significance in their professional pursuits. They ask tough questions about their career paths: *Is this something that adds worth to my life? Is this something that is making a difference in the lives of others? Is this something that is impacting my community for the good?* "But," you say, "I'm not a leader. This stuff doesn't apply to me." Remember the place of influence on the inverted pyramid? If you are there, then you are a self-leader. So at some point in our lives we are all leaders. We either lead ourselves down a destructive, undisciplined path, or we make an impact because we are disciplined self-leaders—ready to pour into others.

Consider this article excerpt concerning great leaders:

Great leaders—whether they lead entire organizations or groups within them—leave a legacy that transcends them and cements their contribution to the growth and transformation of their organization. How they close out their tenure has a lasting impact. As their term of influence grows shorter, leaders must channel their energy, hopes, and fears toward helping their successor and the team they leave behind. This will help the next leader be ready on Day One.

In this article I love the word *transcends*. When someone pursues a venture that transcends them, they are desiring to do something that goes beyond self—something that touches others, inspiring or aiding them to do something equally transcendent.

John D. Rockefeller, often referred to as the richest man in history, looked beyond himself toward what he could do for others. A famous philanthropist and innovator, Rockefeller achieved unbelievable success. A portion of his immense legacy is the University of Chicago. He had a vision for a university that would rival the best in the world and even modeled the architecture after Oxford University in England.

The University of Chicago is considered one of the top global universities, renowned for its dedication to rigorous study and intellectual integrity. It is a part of Rockefeller's legacy. It transcends the man, inspiring and equipping thousands of people who themselves have become world leaders and innovators. That is a legacy that truly transcends the days of a life.

Legacy Hero

Obviously we are not all Rockefellers. But we all have something to give that can benefit others; we all have something that can add to the common good. My friend Lane understands the idea of legacy and its relationship to success. Lane openly admits struggling with the fact that he wanted more out of life than just canned success. He wanted his work to have personal and social impact. He desired to do something that transcended him and touched others—something that would make a lasting imprint on culture.

Lane worked on a legacy-creating idea called Hero Care for three years before he saw it materialize as successful and significant. Hero Care is a nonprofit organization that specializes in providing community heroes—first responders, teachers, armed forces—with specialized home lending, real estate, insurance, financial planning, home construction, and a variety of other services.

Lane explained: "9/11 was the catalyst event that prompted me to start Hero Care. I began thinking about people in my community who did things that really mattered—you know, the people who are actually shaping our society, like public servants. My grandfather was a police officer, so I've had that kind of influence throughout my life.

"But people like my grandfather largely go unnoticed in our culture. We are so busy lavishing rock stars and professional athletes with millions of dollars that we forget the people who make lasting impact."

Hero Care was Lane's way of making his current career transcendent. "I took a step back and thought about my daughter's teacher. She has more influence and spends more time with my daughter than anyone. Yet her time sacrifice is greatly underappreciated. I wanted to change that."

Filling a Void

But where do you find something you can latch on to as Lane did? How do you find something that will leave a legacy?

These are good questions, albeit ones seldom asked. The truth is, only a handful of people seek out transcendent ventures that will leave a lasting impact. Most people never separate themselves from the society dross. Most want to blend in, stay the course, and finish life in one piece. In the sports world, this is known as playing not to lose. Building legacy, however, is for people who play to win—the prize being lasting significance beyond one lifetime.

Lane gave us an excellent paradigm to explore. His approach was simple: find a need and fill it with skills and a business model he already knew.

We don't always have to journey to the far reaches of the planet to find what stirs our passions. Often legacy endeavors stem from passions and desires we have nurtured our entire lives. For Lane, it was a combination of a horrific event that highlighted the real heroes of society and then realizing those heroes are with us every day—even in our families—with the same needs we all share.

As you think through the tension between making your mark and leaving your legacy, consider your life experience and life passions. What have you always been drawn to? What recurring themes do you see along your life's time line? When we focus so much on making a mark along our career paths, we tend to relinquish the idea of lasting significance. Legacy, to us, is a far-away concept left to retirees and dead guys. When we give significance a pass, we diminish our mark in the now.

Remember, one begets the other; either we strive for legacy by being intentional every day or we short-circuit our impact now and are content to be, at best, a flash in the pan—fiery hot but quickly extinguished.

Look around you. What have you always done well? What gets you so excited you do it on your time off? It may be that you simply need to rededicate yourself to your current job and career path. Maybe you're caught up in complacency and need a lift. Take some time to revisit the reasons you chose your current path, and renew your passions for it. You would be surprised at how much of a difference a renewed mind and heart can make in how you approach your work. Many times the difference between that pan flash and lasting legacy is as slight as latent desire. Reignite yourself and watch your legacy build.

Worthwhile Legacy Does Not Just Happen

"In the process of developing Hero Care, there were several times along the journey when I had to stop putting my focus on it and focus on my mortgage business to make money. In pursuing my passion—something

I thought would be my legacy—I still had to bring home the bacon."
Lane's words ring true for so many of us.

Initiating a start-up is not an exact science, especially when it's in
the housing industry. Lane had to walk the tightrope carefully as he
pursued his passion while covering his financial responsibilities with
his daily job. In light of the recent setbacks the economy has endured,
you can imagine that at times Lane's journey was a roller coaster.

Most of us do not fall into the perfect job that will translate into our
lifelong legacy. Like Lane, we must put in the hard work to pave the way
for opportunities, and even fund them. Being in the mortgage business in
recent years, Lane faced heavy setbacks. The crumbling housing market
in Florida (and then nationwide) put the squeeze on him financially, forcing him to take a step toward what he calls his "garage legacy project."

"This idea of mine—Hero Care—was not financially operational in
the early stages," Lane recounted. "It was my garage project. As the
housing market ramped up and then back down, I slowly built upon
my idea until it finally sprouted wings."

Lane flexed his time according to the housing market. When things
were going well, he took advantage of his business opportunities—
shelving Hero Care for a bit. When the market took a dip, he took
advantage of the slack time and continued building his garage project.
Many people are quick to spout off ideas on why they cannot pursue
the things they care about most. But in the end, we all make our own
decisions and are the final governors of our time.

Lane was inspired, he had an idea he could throw himself into, and
he went for it. Self-discipline is the only difference between Lane and
other people who are content to complain about their lack of time.

But life is full of disruptors. Outside of our work lives we have lives
of constant interruption. Instead of cultivating a lifestyle of discovery,
we are content to feed our material lusts without a second thought.
Lane would retreat to his garage to shape his dream and his thoughts,

forgoing evenings on the couch watching television. Instead of trips to the mall, he dedicated his time to Hero Care—an investment that would pay dividends as he finally made it a sustaining enterprise.

Shaping Culture with Legacy

Our culture is not shaped by the masses. It is shaped by a small percentage of people chasing more than comfortable houses and status quo lifestyles. Think about all of the major brands and organizations you love: Starbucks, Nike, One. Dynamic people founded these companies. They chased transcendent ideas. They pursued ventures that went further than merely selling items. They sold ideals—they incited inspiration.

Let's look at Starbucks, for example. Great coffee and a great environment in which to enjoy coffee with your friends is what made them great. They became the proverbial "third place." When you think of a café to hang out in or a meeting place to get coffee, you think of Starbucks.

As their growth burgeoned, however, they strayed away from what made them great. The focus drifted from coffee. They started carrying more retail items, so the stores became more about selling goods than providing that great place to come meet with friends and have a cup of coffee.

Company founder Howard Shultz knew that, in order to preserve what made the company great to begin with, they would have to do an about-face. Today Starbucks is making serious concessions—giving customers a say in how the business is run, being more thoughtful in how they handle retail—in order to satisfy their loyal customer base and to highlight what made them great to begin with: outstanding coffee.

Business ventures like these are expressions of people who refused to settle, people who overcame great odds—people who view significance and legacy as their mark. They set their goals based upon a future outcome, not an immediate result. We are drawn to these businesses and products because we, too, want to be associated with transcendent ideas. We want to feel we are part of something that sets trends instead of follows them; we want to be viewed as progressive.

How will you shape culture, which is the current of transcendence? What will you sacrifice in order to produce something that flows to the next generation and beyond? If you remain shortsighted and results oriented your whole life, you will have your reward in the immediate. But if you apply your passion to your ingenuity, then you can have a hand in shaping the way people experience life every day and into the future. Like Lane with Hero Care, you can begin creating new avenues for ideas and processes that we do not even know we need yet. The following insights will prove valuable.

Insight #1: Differentiate Yourself from the Common

Legacy can be intimidating to talk about. All of a sudden the pressure is on to produce something spectacular and innovative. But it doesn't have to be this way. It just takes focus—laser focus.

When I spoke with Lane about Hero Care, he told me the progression of events that led to his initial *aha* moment. "Hero Care evolved from my desire to meet needs that I saw. In 2005 I read *Blue Ocean Strategy*, by W. Chan Kim and Renee Mauborgne, and realized that I needed to differentiate myself from the rest of the mortgage industry."

Lane continued, "One of the main things I picked up in the book was that I needed to look at similar offerings in other industries. Why just offer specialized home financing to heroes?"

Then things started to crystallize for Lane. "I was in Park City, Utah, pitching my idea to a group of professionals, when I really started getting great feedback. After the presentation people were coming up to me and telling me that my idea was one that needed to be replicated all over the country—they were telling me the idea was incredible. That was when I began to realize that this idea was bigger than a mere specialized mortgage company.

"This business model was something completely new. The people we were helping were part of some of the largest employers in the country. I was tapping into massive networks with nearly unlimited potential. To top it all off, it was serving a great need in the community. I had found the thing to build my legacy on."

Differentiation is a key component to any successful business. But few people apply the concept to their own pursuits. Lane was embedded in an industry where everyone played from the same deck of cards. To stay in an industry where he felt comfortable, he had to rise above the commonness of it all and stand out.

By attaching "care" to his new endeavor, Lane began to turn heads. When he finally made the decision to transform it from a for-profit business into a nonprofit, things really started to roll. People were not getting bogged down with questions about who was gaining financially from it all. Instead, they were getting excited about the idea and spreading the word. Lane took the ordinary and made it extraordinary by pouring himself into an otherwise mundane industry and recasting it as something that sought the greater good for others.

Here are some points to consider about your own position as you think through Lane's situation:

- Are you trapped in "the ordinary" of your industry? If so, how can you pry yourself away?
- Can you reinvent your current industry to transcend typical outcome models?
- What ideas are keeping you up at night? Perhaps you need to pursue something else entirely. You can also differentiate yourself by doing something that no one else is doing in your community. What steps can you take to move daily toward pursuing your legacy full-time?

- Who can you assemble as your personal focus group? Unique ideas are often born out of collaboration.
- What are you most gifted and passionate about? Do not get bogged down with a multitude of ideas. Chase down the one thing you could see yourself doing as a labor of love and start shaping it.

Insight #2: Omit the Interruptions

Forming a legacy will demand your personal time and resources. Moving from merely making your mark to pursuing lasting significance is a process that requires your full attention. This may require a major lifestyle overhaul.

Earlier in this chapter we discussed how culture creates barriers to life-fulfilling pursuits. You must figure out which interruptions keep you from pursuing significance. This is not an easy thing to do. We all enjoy our life routines. In fact, being entrenched in the everyday grind is an appealing and comfortable rut. But you have decided that you are not one of those people. You want to leave more than a mark in your current role—you want to be part of something greater than you are, something with the potential to grow on its own because other people will fight to be part of it.

The assumption I am working on is that you have a desire to leave a legacy. You are not content simply to leave your mark in your career field. You want to be part of something that lasts, and if you have things your way, you want to build it from the bottom up. In order to do this you have to cut the fat—get rid of the interruptions in your life.

Here is a short list of actionable steps you can take now to maximize your time and build toward your legacy:

- *Cut wasteful time with the television.* With the exception of gathering with friends to watch the big game, television saps time like nothing else.

You can burn two hours without even thinking about it—and that's just cable news. A Deloitte survey reported that adults ages twenty-six to forty-two spend an average of fifteen hours a week watching television. The next age bracket, thirty-three to sixty-one, watches more than twenty hours of television per week.[1] The older we get, the more time we waste in front of the tube—or big flat LCD box (times are changing!).

Television can be a great way to relax with your family, but too often the television dictates the family's schedule. This should never happen. Reclaim your time and limit your viewing times to shows that matter most. Sacrificing a few programs could buy six to ten hours a week that you can dedicate to writing out your business proposal or meeting with colleagues to discuss your idea.

- *Become an early riser.* Okay, stop rolling your eyes. Yes, we have all heard the axiom about early to bed and early to rise. But you would be surprised how much work you can get done in the early morning hours when everyone else is sleeping. Getting up at six in the morning three times a week will allow you to stay on top of your current workload and give you spare time to make calls or research your brilliant idea.

  If you simply cannot do mornings, then shoot for a few late coffee nights. You may pay for it in the morning, but some of the most creative ideas come after the clock strikes midnight. At least that's what a few of my friends say.

- *Schedule and take advantage of days off.* This one will vary in its application, depending on your family situation. This is headed in the same general direction as the first two steps: become a better steward of your time. On Saturdays you could implement your new "early riser" idea and use that time for brainstorming sessions at the local Starbucks. If you have a few personal days per year, dedicate time during those days to forming your new plan.

Remember Lane's "garage" project. He worked on it when he could. When things were up in the housing market, he worked hard to get ahead. When they were down, he used that time to his advantage. By strategically using your days off, you can dictate and schedule time spent on your project. Like Lane, you are stewarding your time wisely, but in this scenario you are in control.

- *Give yourself deadlines.* I know plenty of people with great ideas. But the people who move on those ideas are the ones who take the time to write out a time line—deadlines for deliverables. This takes an extraordinary amount of self-discipline, but you can do it. In fact, if you are really passionate about your idea, a deadline gives you the discipline. It's like a budget—when you operate within a budget, you actually experience more freedom with your money because you have clear parameters for how to use it. The same applies to deadlines. They provide you with a clear destination—a goal to strive for. Setting deadlines then becomes a huge motivating factor in your life.

Say, for example, you have a great idea for a book that will turn your industry upside down. It's not enough to sit with your colleagues and muse about how great your idea is. You must take action. Begin writing the overview for your book. Look up online what publishers expect in a book proposal. Then give yourself a deadline for having the proposal finished. A deadline will help you minimize everyday interruptions and keep you on task to complete the job on time.

Many people dislike deadlines, citing that they hinder creativity and insert too much stress into a project. But this is false. When you have a goal to work toward, you automatically become inspired to meet that deadline and have a clear vision for where you are headed. If you need help, ask a good friend to keep you accountable once a week. Remember, if you don't take steps toward producing a tangible result for your great idea, someone else will.

- *Get involved with worthwhile causes.* Yes, this is an interruption, but it's a purposeful interruption. Getting involved in your community allows you to get your finger on the heartbeat of everyone around you. What are people concerned about? What are they wishing for? Who are the leaders in the community? You can discover the true needs of your community just by getting involved, listening to others, and lending a hand.

    As an added bonus, you will receive more than you give—as is always the case with getting involved in causes that are doing a good work. By opening yourself up and helping those in need, you gain an immeasurable experience that may even become the impetus for your new endeavor—your legacy.

Leaving a Legacy

When I was finishing my discussion with Lane, he became extremely passionate about this whole concept of leaving a legacy. I asked him if he could look professionals in the eye and give them some advice, what would it be? Here is what he said:

If you want to make your life matter, consider this: you spend most of your life working, and if life is really all about leaving a legacy, then you must invest your work hours in something that will contribute to leaving a legacy.

If you have a family, outside of work time there is little time left to build a legacy. You can have a garage passion, a moonlighting passion, but you will rarely be in the life scenario to support a full-scale effort. Doing something significant with your life takes time, resources, and energy. You can't expect to accomplish it with a part-time mentality—you must go all in. You have to learn to transition your work into your investment for legacy. That is the key.

Lane brings up some excellent points of tension. Seeking a job that will leave a legacy is not a simple task. If you are fortunate enough to find something that speaks your language, how do you make the transition from a nice, consistent salary to something that only promises risk—but has the potential to fulfill you? How do you pull the trigger in that situation?

Even though it's not a simple decision, it's simple in scope in that it forces you to weigh serious life circumstances against a dream you can't be sure will come to fruition. That is to say, you either decide to pursue significance in your career or you do not. If you can't commit to the dream, you're still obligated to do the best in your current situation.

Conversely, if you are balancing your garage project with your real job, you must stay dialed in to your current employer. Lane described this tension as "building a career you are passionate about while making a mark in your current job." You can't be in all places all the time—thus, the idea of harmonizing the pursuit of legacy with the now of your current work. As we discussed in Insight #2, it's about stewarding your time. You have to decide to pursue legacy, then you need to tighten the bolts in your personal and professional life to see the project through as Lane did.

I recently spoke with a young friend of mine in his early thirties who has decided to return to graduate school. He described his juggling act to me—it was intense. His goal—his legacy-leaving idea—is to one day become a writer and professor so he can inspire and instruct young people. His goal is noble, but the road there is not going to be easy. As many of us do, he has a mortgage, a growing family, and a full-time job to hold down while attending classes on weekends and reading the nights away.

It will be a season that will make demands on his relationships, his finances, and his will to succeed in his endeavor. But the reward of his hard work will be worth it. He is pursuing significance—something greater than himself—and that is what drives him every day.

The same can be true for you. Perhaps you are on the fence right now trying to decide whether or not to pursue an idea that has been brewing for months or years. Maybe you fear the risk involved in taking that step toward legacy. Is it too much to ask of you at this moment? Will you be able to handle the pressure of being involved at your current work while pursuing the thing that really embodies your passions? There are no easy answers for these questions.

Remember the words of C. S. Lewis: "The pain now is part of the pleasure then." He knew that whatever a person goes through in the present will be a part of the future in some fashion. For you, now is your time to push ahead and develop your idea—moving toward legacy. The road will be dangerous and difficult to navigate, but the destination is reward in all its glory. Your pain now will be part of the joy then.

Making your mark in the now is temporary. Legacy goes much deeper than a career mark. It is the culmination of a life in pursuit of significance.

Harmony in the Legacy

If life were just about work, then the idea of self-realization would not matter. We would simply all pursue whatever brought in the most money and gave us the best creature comforts money could buy. But this is not reality.

The very fact that most people reading this book have, at some point, felt that deep need to do something more in life—to seek a deeper purpose—testifies to the reality that we were all born for legacy. But in order to get to the point of leaving something significant behind for your family and coworkers, you must become adept at finding harmony in the monotony of earning your wage combined with the weight of pursuing something that has lasting impact.

To be in balance is to be in tension. The tightrope walker does not find a magical equilibrium and rest in it. He fights to the right and then to the left, until at long last he is across the wire and safe on the other side. This is you in life. Work beckons you along and, at times, offers you the means to have things that culture deems indicative of success.

But this is a façade. Our culture would sell you a bridge in the Sahara if you were willing to finance it. The point is that material and financial success solve only a portion of the puzzle. The other parts are what give you purpose—what drive you and bring you the most joy. Those other parts contain your passions and dreams. You would do anything to see them come to fruition. These are the parts that pull you along and force you to keep asking questions, to keep wondering if there is something more.

It is this work/life tension that ultimately makes your life dynamic—separating you from the others who are content to remain static. Legacy is not static; it is born out of the invigorations of men and women just like you, who dare to try to do what is welling up inside of them.

Think of every person you know who has left a legacy. Do you view them as a static person? Of course not. You are drawn to them because their lives are in a constant state of flux. Their lives are ebbing and flowing in and out of work and dreams and family and fun and travel and spontaneity. No one wants to be stuck in a plush New York studio condo with all the fancy fixings and no one to share it with.

Balancing Act

How do you stay balanced on the wire *and* build your legacy? The fact that anyone is purposefully grabbing some life during the workweek is a testament that something deeper is at work in them—or that they are just plain irresponsible (but that is not an option in our discussion).

The deeper current is a clear understanding by those individuals who know they must input in order to output—they must be a complete person before they can help others realize how to reach the same understanding.

The 10:00 a.m. snorkelers were proactive; they understood that in order for them to perform at optimum levels they had to create a purposeful imbalance during their week. Take another look at the inverted pyramid. The top section is the pinnacle of personal and professional success. The diagram shows this zenith in life when you have impact. But not just any kind of impact—not impact that is over and done. Lasting impact.

A lasting impact is possible only if you remain vigilant in your efforts to keep incorporating diverse experiences into your normal life routine. Another application is the more practical idea of establishing a healthy work/life tension. You cannot get caught making decisions in the now that do not build your legacy.

Of course this harmonic perspective is only possible when you are beginning from a place of self-realization. In order to make decisions that will also affect your legacy, you must have a clear understanding of self.

The Harmonic Perspective of Legacy

- Clear understanding of self
- Clear understanding of personal and professional direction
- Clear understanding of how you plan to achieve personal/professional goals
- Clear understanding of current professional context
- Clear understanding of the needs of others (personal, professional)

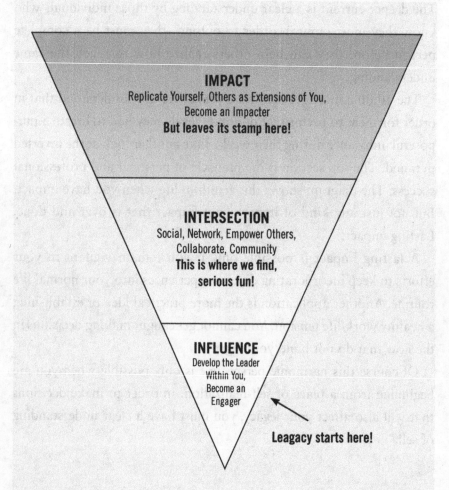

IMPACT
Replicate Yourself, Others as Extensions of You,
Become an Impacter
But leaves its stamp here!

INTERSECTION
Social, Network, Empower Others,
Collaborate, Community
**This is where we find,
serious fun!**

INFLUENCE
Develop the Leader
Within You,
Become an
Engager

Leagacy starts here!

Making Good Decisions vs. Managing Decisions Already Made

Decisions help us start. Discipline helps us finish.

—John C. Maxwell

There is one thing that will keep you at the top—the decisions you make.

—Todd Duncan

It Falls on You

You are in the process of creating a masterpiece. Every day there is an opportunity to improve. The most successful people change their lives because they can see the opportunity to change something today. You are an agent of change, and your life and your business are both your responsibility and your opportunity. In summarizing this book and the stories and ideas contained between its covers, there are five consistent truths about all people that are important to understand before we take on making and managing decisions.

1. Most people are not as happy as they could or should be. The key to happiness is improving who you are and how you live.

2. Most people do not have a plan in the present that helps them effectively navigate toward their future.

3. Most people are locked into the limiting belief that this is their lot in life, that they can't get anywhere beyond where they are.

4. Most people want a different reality but are not committed to the action it will take to create it.

5. Most people are not living up to their potential—they let their current reality define them instead of destine them.

Make Each Day Your Masterpiece

As I looked at the autographed basketball and Pyramid of Success John Wooden gave me, I was reminded that he constantly instructed his players to make each day their masterpiece:

> When I was teaching basketball, I urged my players to try their hardest to improve on that very day, to make that practice a masterpiece. Too often we get distracted by what is outside our control. You can't do anything about yesterday. The door to the past has been shut and the key thrown away. You can do nothing about tomorrow. It is yet to come. However, tomorrow is in large part determined by what you do today. So make today a masterpiece . . . This rule is even more important in life than in basketball. You have to apply yourself every day to become a little better. By applying yourself to the task of becoming a little bit better each and every day over a period of time, you will become a lot better. Only then will you be able to approach being the best you can be.[1]

Masterpieces are created when you make good decisions and then commit to managing those decisions. Both require you to master the art of self-leadership and embrace the importance of self-discipline.

How would the person you see yourself becoming in the future be acting today, in the present? I love this question. I ask it of myself often. It brings immediate perspective to each aspect of life. You will never change your life or your business if you don't manage yourself every day. You will never move from the base of Maslow's pyramid to become a fully engaged human being without self-leadership.

Making Discipline Your Mantra Makes You Feel Good

Self-leadership is daily discipline. Purposeful imbalance comes from determining your daily plan based on the decisions you have made, then managing that plan. In almost every case where there is a failure to operate in the tension of purposeful imbalance, it comes either from not making critical decisions or not managing the daily decisions that were made at a point in time.

You are going somewhere. I'm going somewhere. The question is where? And then the decision must be made to manage your daily agenda. Leadership guru and dear friend John Maxwell said it like this:

You begin to build a better life by determining to make good decisions, but that alone is not enough. You need to know what decisions to make. I've given the subject a lot of thought, talked to many successful people, and narrowed the list of critical areas for success to twelve. I call them the Daily Dozen:

1. Attitude: Choose and display the right attitudes daily.
2. Priorities: Determine and act on important priorities daily.
3. Health: Know and follow healthy guidelines daily.
4. Family: Communicate and care for my family daily.
5. Thinking: Practice and develop good thinking daily.
6. Commitment: Make and keep proper commitments daily.
7. Finances: Make and properly manage dollars daily.

8. Faith: Deepen and live out my faith daily.

9. Relationships: Initiate and invest in solid relationships daily.

10. Generosity: Plan for and model generosity daily.

11. Values: Embrace and practice good values daily.

12. Growth: Seek and experience improvements daily.

If you settle these twelve issues by making the right decision in each area and then manage those decisions daily, you can be successful.[2]

I look at most of the times in my life when things were not going right, and I can tie every challenge and problem and setback and failure to one of these twelve areas. Either I didn't make the decisions necessary for success, or I had made the decisions but didn't harness my self-discipline to manage them. Both are bad. One leads to lack of clarity, and one leads to lack of action. Both chip away at self-esteem, and personal integrity starts to slip away, creating the downward spiral and perpetual reversal of all things good and well.

What is integrity in this sense? Integrity is best defined by the concept of self-leadership. Dr. Pamela Butler said, "There is no person with whom you spend more time than any other, a person who has more influence over you, and more ability to interfere with or to support your growth than anyone else. This ever-present companion is your own self." Essentially, the management of your own being is the critical factor in the management of the decisions you make.

In his book *The Psychology of Self-Esteem*, psychological theorist Nathaniel Branden said, "Productive work is the process through which man achieves that sense of control over his life which is the production of his being able to fully enjoy the other values possible to him." This then is the key: balance is the by-product of making decisions and then controlling the factors that consistently invade and interrupt the successful and consistent management of those decisions.

The direct relationship between our sense of self-worth and our personal productivity is a relatively new concept in life management. In time management, because its basis is personal productivity, the relationship is vital. A person may possess many practical skills and be able to apply them well and yet have a very low self-esteem. This person may feel a great discomfort at the thought of having to learn a new skill or having to change his or her environment in any meaningful way.

Another person with a high self-esteem may be lacking in practical skills, but having no fear of learning or of confronting a new environment, he or she can quickly and enjoyably learn and adapt to different situations. In the latter example, the person had confidence in his or her ability—based on a healthy self-esteem.

Purposeful imbalance requires self-leadership, but self-leadership cannot be engaged before asking new questions. New questions serve one key purpose—they make our imaginations come alive. The most important decisions will begin with and spring forth from an internal emotion that often lies dormant. Questions that are both heart- and head-provoking can begin to move an individual to a position of possibilities. The following are some of the questions from our Life Planning series.

- What if I could go home on time? I could save more? I could spend more time with my family? I could get that promotion? I could become self-employed? What are my dreams and desires? What if I could achieve these?
- What would need to happen to take my life to a whole new level? My business? My career?
- What decision could be made in the next five minutes, and what action could be taken in the next sixty minutes, to create fulfillment and happiness in the _____ [state area] of my life?
- What am I not willing to settle for any longer in my life? In my business? In my finances? In my health? In my relationships?
- Which areas of my life are most stressful for me? Why? What hope lies ahead in helping reduce the stress in that environment?

- What could I say no to that would give me more margin or freedom with my time?

These questions evoke "heart of heart" emotions. They help center our thinking on new decisions. They give us the chance to formulate plans and to develop new habits. But the answers to our questions won't mean a thing unless we are committed to taking action consistently in the areas of change we desire.

Start Small, Start Now

All new growth requires new decisions and action, and there will never be new growth if you procrastinate. But change is hard; the bigger it is the more likely it will feel intimidating. That's why I like "chunking things down." Starting small is easier than starting big. And starting now is better than waiting. My friend and colleague Dick Biggs, author of *Burn Brightly Without Burning Out*, said, "The greatest gap in life is the one between knowing and doing."

If we want to change and grow, we all know deep down that we must get started. Yet, procrastination has become the great friend of many. I found this in my files from a guy named Sammy Poole:

So Stop Waiting . . .

Until your car or home is paid off.
Until you get a new car or home.
Until your kids leave the house.
Until you go back to school.
Until you finish school.
Until you lose ten pounds.
Until you gain ten pounds.

Until you get married.

Until you get a divorce.

Until you have kids.

Until you retire.

Until summer.

Until spring.

Until winter.

Until fall.

Until you die.

What's holding you back? Why have you procrastinated? While there may be a million reasons you haven't started, there is only one reason why you should start: it's your life!

You will be somewhere in the future. On your current course, what will you look back on and wish you had started? What regrets might you have? Whatever the answer, the first decision you must make is to start—to begin. Once in motion, then you're on your way, self-leadership takes over, and your new decisions become your reality.

There are six governing principles of self-leadership that will give you a sense of control over the decisions you make and give you the discipline to back those decisions.

Principle #1:
Self-leadership means knowing
what's important to you.

Make clarity your commitment.

Do you know what makes you tick? Do you have a grip on what drives you to wake up every morning and keep doing what you are doing? I have spoken to many people in different seasons of life who tell me they feel as if they're living in a fog. They just cannot seem to find a clear vision for their lives.

The reason they lack a clear vision is because they do not know what is most important to them. The fog comes from pursuing success apart from purpose. Albert Einstein said, "Try not to become a man of success, but rather, try to become a man of values." Clarity comes from knowing; from a healthy self-knowledge we develop core values based upon what is important to us—what our purpose is.

In order to *do* you must first *know.* In the movie *The Matrix,* the ultimate believer, Morpheus, tells Neo (the One) that there is a difference between knowing the path and walking the path. Neo could not live a life indicative of the One without first knowing and coming to grips with the fact that he *was* the One.

Likewise, you cannot walk the path of life and expect to perform to your full potential unless you understand what is important to you. The following principles are moot if you cannot define this first one. Ask yourself, *What is important to me?* When you can answer this, you can then set out on a path that always keeps that answer at the forefront. It defines your path.

Norman Vincent Peale said this about knowing your purpose:

We are to be excited from youth to old age, to have an insatiable curiosity about the world . . . We are also here to help others by practicing a friendly attitude. And every person is born for a purpose. Everyone has a God-given potential, in essence, built into him or her. And if we are to live life to the fullest, we must realize that potential.

Principle #2:
Self-leadership means scheduling
what's important to you.

Make prioritization your passion.

If you do not take control of your schedule, it will take control of you. Stephen Covey put it this way: "The key is not to prioritize what's on your schedule but to schedule your priorities." In this high-productivity world we often forget that there comes a time when we need to unplug. Work spills over into family. Family gets neglected. Stress builds and relationships—the ones closest to you— become strained.

You must learn to schedule time with your loved ones first and foremost. I have friends who schedule their lunch breaks so that it shows up busy on their calendars. I have other friends who schedule time with their kids during the workweek; when something work-related comes up, they simply fall back on their calendar that says "Football with Billy" or "Lunch Date with Madison."

If you have a family, that is your first priority. Once your family is taken care of, then schedule accordingly. Prioritizing is essential to knowing what gets scheduled and what you say no to. The great German writer and philosopher Goethe said it best: "Things that matter most must never be at the mercy of things which matter least."

Principle #3:
Self-leadership means doing
what's important to you.

Make action your asset.

Don't be the type of person who goes through life living for someone else. When you perform just to please others, you can get caught in a trap that steals away your identity. If I went through life always allowing my priorities and passions to be defined by others, I would cease to be the person I was meant to be. I pursue the things most important to me because I believe they were placed inside of me at birth. Throughout my life they have been refined and honed to be what they are today. I do what is important to me because those things define my purpose.

But you cannot keep your eye on the important things in life without a heavy dose of discipline and positive self-speak. You have to live on purpose, striving for your purpose, believing that your purpose matters and will ultimately give you deep self-worth. The teacher in the book of Proverbs said, "He who neglects discipline despises himself" (15:32 NASB).

The wisdom here is simple: if you are not intentional about pursuing what is important to you, then you lack discipline, which makes you a self-despiser instead of a self-leader. This passage by my friend Og Mandino says it all:

I will act now. I will act now. I will act now. Henceforth, I will repeat these words each hour, each day, every day, until the words become as much a habit as my breathing; and the action, which follows, becomes as instinctive as the blinking of my eyelids. With these words I can condition my mind to perform every action necessary for my success. I will act now.

I will repeat these words again and again and again. I will walk where failures fear to walk. I will work when failures seek rest. I will act now for now is all I have.

Tomorrow is the day reserved for the labor of the lazy. I am not lazy. Tomorrow is the day when the failure will succeed. I am not a failure. I will act now. Success will not wait. If I delay, success will become wed to another and lost to me forever. This is the time. This is the place. I am the person.

Principle #4:
Self-leadership means completing what's important to you.

Make finishing your focus.

If you have ever participated in team sports, you have probably heard a coach say, "It's not how you start, it's how you finish." This is excellent advice—not just for a game, but for life. We all know the person with the ideas, always spinning a web and starting things but never seeing it to fruition. This is poor self-leadership.

This principle dovetails nicely with Principle #3 in that it takes discipline to *do* what is important to you, but it also takes discipline to see those things through. It has been said, "We rate ability in men by what they finish, not by what they attempt." So true. You do not get Brownie points for ideas that sit on your to-do list. And you certainly do not receive accolades for the project you started but then shelved for lack of discipline.

The strong self-leader knows how to finish and finish strong. He is governed by a confident passion that stems from his clear vision of what matters most to him. He is a person of values. Because he has such a clear vision, he knows how to schedule his life in a way that empowers him to achieve tasks designed around his strengths. His clarity and passion are key to finishing a project. If you want to be coached by the best, then listen to John Wooden: "It's not so important who starts the game but who finishes."

Principle #5:
Self-leadership means evaluating how you are doing in the areas that are important to you.

Make improvement your initiative.

Self-evaluation is not easy to learn, nor is it easy to do. It takes true humility to admit that things may not be going so well—that you are off course. But self-evaluation is a key asset to sound self-leadership. It is something that never really ends but that continues to develop over time. John Maxwell said, "Success is a continuing thing. It is growth and development. It is achieving one thing and using that as a stepping-stone to achieve something else."

In order to achieve and move on to something else, you must be able to evaluate your progress. The strong leaders are the ones who are always making improvements in their personal and professional lives so that one harmonizes with the other. Achieving professional success doesn't mean that you've arrived; rather, it means that you're always moving toward your next project, your next opportunity for success. As Winston Churchill asserted, "Success is never final." What about you? Are you simply living for temporary success? A true self-leader is always striving to better his or her craft, to grow as a person, and to find success in whatever avenue presents itself.

Principle #6:
Self-leadership means learning
from your mistakes.

Make failure your friend.

Self-evaluation means nothing if you cannot learn from your mistakes. By confronting your mistakes you take one step closer to becoming the person you are supposed to be. None of us would be anywhere without self-evaluation.

I once heard a coach compare the athlete who can self-evaluate with the one who can't think past the current play. An athlete who is self-evaluating is usually your captain. He or she is the athlete who understands how mistakes (especially his or hers) affect the momentum and outcome of the game. If an athlete cannot make adjustments during a game, then chances are the athlete will lose. It is the same outside of the game.

In business or in personal life, it's easy to spot someone who keeps running into the same brick wall. They make the same mistakes because they refuse to learn from their mistakes. In sports it's the athlete who can make adjustments during play or at halftime or between holes who will typically rise above the competition. Too often when people face defeat, they respond either by never trying again or by continuing their faulty strategy or action.

Napoleon Hill, author of *Think and Grow Rich,* said, "When defeat comes, accept it as a signal that your plans are not sound, rebuild those plans, and set sail once more toward your coveted goal." What great advice! Learn from your mistake. Your plan is not sound, so make corrections and get back in the game.

The Power of Accountability

No one individual is as strong as many together. You've heard Proverbs 17:17: "As iron sharpens iron, so one man sharpens another." But how many of us really implement this in our personal and professional lives? The concept is accountability. I am better because others make me so. I accomplish things because I surround myself with people who speak truth into my life—who keep me *accountable* to my goals and commitments.

But many of us fear accountability for different reasons. Some fear the success that may come from it. Others doubt that they can even be successful, so why bother. Still others simply procrastinate: "I'll work on my masterpiece tomorrow."

The fact is that if we truly desire our personal and professional lives to be masterpieces, if we really seek to improve ourselves and move toward our goals, then we must engage in accountability.

Accountability is the final element that makes the discipline of self-leadership possible. Accountability in your professional life gives you a coach, someone to help you plan your goals and set expectations for your career. In your personal life accountability means that all your decisions revolve around the standards that you set. These decisions, then, are informed—not haphazardly decided. They adhere to your life purpose. But this kind of accountability is only possible if you allow inclusion for those whom you trust. Accountability does not happen in a vacuum.

Similar to personal accountability is the kind that you share with your spouse. It is deep and intimate. It should be at a level where your partner knows your plans and can help you shape your daily action. All facets of accountability involve people—others speaking reason, truth, and hard love into your life.

But there is also another kind of accountability to be developed: prayerful accountability. This is wisdom that you draw from during times of solitude and deep reflection. It is in these great moments of solitude that you will find your most profound moves toward significance. Whether you are receiving accountability from a person, a group, or the fruits of prayerful solitude, you will gain the rewards that come from this element of self-discipline.

You will begin to make better choices by allowing others to shape you and add value to your life. You will become the wise man or woman who seeks the counsel of others. But not just anyone's counsel; you are receiving input from trusted colleagues and family members and friends.

Along with better choices you will gain the wisdom of discretion. Our discretion grows when we weigh behaviors, reactions, and daily decisions that shape our personal and professional lives. And with discretion comes sharper, more defined actions.

As leaders we are constantly in front of those we lead and those we seek to lead. Accountability helps to shape our actions—the by-products of wise counsel and discretion. Critic and essayist Marya Mannes said, "It's not enough to show people how to live better; there is a mandate for any person or group with enormous powers of communication to show people *how* to be better."

Do you see the building blocks forming here? Accountability is a foundation for self-discipline because it builds the self. So the progression continues. As we model wise leadership we build our self-respect. We become stronger individuals because we are connected to a core of others. Like the strand of rope that King Solomon talked about in the book of Proverbs, that connection is not easily broken. But when we are isolated—as one strand—we become weak and easily torn in two.

Yet from this tight strand we begin to adapt the qualities of those we are stranded together with. We will also be challenged in our minds to think deeply about new ideas and concepts. Others can challenge our preconceptions about life and business and family. In this way we form new ideas and are able to creatively assert them into our businesses and personal lives.

Instead of growing at the pace of one, we grow exponentially because we have many voices helping to mold us. All of this ties into the idea of legacy. Strong self-leaders are the ones who, through sound accountability, manage their decisions by being self-disciplined. It all wraps up nicely. But not easily.

Succeeding at accountability is more art than science. I'm not talking about a once a month rap session with some close friends and you. I'm talking about purposeful times of tugging and pulling at one another. Some of the best times of growth in my own life have come from being left on the anvil of accountability to bleed for a while.

Balancing the tensions in life is no easy task. You cannot live life on the wire alone. As Plato said, "Every heart sings a song, incomplete, until another heart whispers back."

In your life, who is whispering back?

The stories we've looked at are examples that life is a great teacher, one that is hard and unforgiving at times. But the lessons we learn as we walk the tightrope will never come easy. The good news comes when we look around and see our personal lives infusing balance into our professional lives and vice-versa.

Henry Drummond said, "Therefore, keep in the midst of life. Do not isolate yourself. Be among men and things, and among troubles, and difficulties, and obstacles." You will find great tension in the midst of life. But it is that great tension that will drive you toward a purposeful imbalance, and it is the power of accountability that will mold you into the kind of self-leader who makes a true impact.

NOTES

Introduction

1. Mayo Clinic staff, "Exercise: Rev up your routine to reduce stress," http://www.mayoclinic.com/health/exercise-and-stress/SR00036.
2. Fast Company
3. "Measuring Stick: A semi-random look at some statistics reflecting our work and lives," *Worthwhile*, September/October 2005, 82–83.

Second Tension Point

1. Tim Sanders, *The Likeability Factor*.

Third Tension Point

1. JF. *Rolling Stone*, 1991.
2. Anna Bahney, "A Life Between Jobs," *New York Times*, June 8, 2006.
3. Polly LaBarre, "How to Lead a Rich Life," *Fast Company*, March 2003.

Fourth Tension Point

1. *Men's Journal*, 2005.

Fifth Tension Point

1. *New York Times*, September 25, 1988.
2. Ibid.

Seventh Tension Point

1. From a transcribed, tape recorded interview of Henry Stein by Martha Edwards on March 28, 1995, in the AAISF/ATP Archives.
2. "East Coker," T. S. Eliot.

3. Tim Sanders, "Love Is the Killer App," *Fast Company*, December 19, 2007, http://www.fastcompany.com/magazine/55/love.html?page=0%2C0.

4. Andy Crouch, *Culture Makers*, IVP.

Eighth Tension Point

1. Sushama Khanna, "Increasing Employee Retention Through Employee Engagement—A Challenge for HR," *Annual Handbook of Human Resource Initiatives 2008*.

2. *The Red Rubber Ball*, Kevin Carol.

3. Patricia Bathurst, "Having fun at work increases loyalty, productivity" *azcentral.com*, June 1, 2008, http://www.azcentral.com/business/articles/2008/06/01/20080601biz-funatwork0601-ON.html.

Ninth Tension Point

1. D. Kirkpatrick, *Fortune Magazine*, June 27, 2005.

2. Gordon MacDonald, *Life At Work* Magazine.

Tenth Tension Point

1. http://www.hollywoodreporter.com/hr/content_display/news/e3ic41d147829e712a6a6ecd990ea3a349c.

The Summit

1. John Wooden with Steve Jamison, *Wooden: A Lifetime of Observations and Reflections On and Off the Court*. Chicago Contemporary Books, 1997, 11–12.

2. John Maxwell, *Make Today Count*. Center Street, 2008, 24.

This book is dedicated to my assistant, Amy Dickens, who for 11 years has helped me live my life on the wire.

I'd like to thank my writers Brent Cole and Tim Willard for helping shape a manuscript we are all very proud of. You guys did a great job.

And I'd like to thank Daniel Harkavy, the founder of Building Champions, for being my life coach and for being by my side since 1994, helping me make smart choices and live a life of purpose.

Time Traps addresses the most common misconceptions we have about time and our use of that time in the marketplace. Duncan has proven remedies for universal time troubles, and he shows readers how to set a schedule that works-not just some days but every day. With the principles in *Time Traps*, business professionals will see a rise in their productivity as they experience a drop in their working hours.

Todd Duncan reveals the 10 most common mistakes salespeople make, and offers insight on how to avoid them. Duncan addresses these catastrophic mistakes with clarity and directness. Whether you're a seasoned sales professional or someone considering sales as a career, Duncan's wisdom can help you avoid errors in perception, practice, and performance that could not only cost you a sale, but also your career.

In *High Trust Selling*, Duncan shows you how to connect who you are and what you are about in your selling career, giving you phenomenal and long-lasting results.

THOMAS NELSON
Since 1798

Printed in the USA
CPSIA information can be obtained
at www.ICGtesting.com
JSHW032333111124
73366JS00019B/317

9 781595 555267